£5

-British-
WARSHIPS
Since 1945

D0807651

Part 3
DESTROYERS
y Mike Critchley

£2.95

THOSE WERE THE DAYS

The 7th Destroyer Squadron — Sliema Creek — Malta 1961

During the war, 278 Destroyers were completed in British yards including both those built for other navies and taken over by the R.N. — and those loaned, transferred, etc to allied navies.

127 Destroyers and 12 leaders — a total of 139 ships — were lost in World War Two. 63 in the Mediterranean and 50 in Home Waters. 47 of those lost had been completed after the outbreak of war.

By 1960 only 52 Destroyers remained in commission out of the 250 in the first half of 1945.

By April, 1964 there were just 9 Destroyers and 5 Fleet Pickets in commission, 22 others being in Reserve or refitting

AUTHOR'S NOTES

In compiling this book it has been extremely difficult to decide what to put in—and what to leave out! As a general rule I have only included ships that had a post war role to fulfil—even if only to remain in the Reserve Fleet for a decade or more! Many ships were scrapped shortly after the end of the war and have been deliberately omitted.

In researching this book I have found some ships have left behind them a wealth of material to record their activities—others have quietly disappeared leaving very little paperwork behind them! As always happens I will, no doubt, have letters from my readers "filling in the gaps" I have been unable to fill—if only I could find these good people before a book goes to print!

Without the help received from Lt Cdr Ken Burns DSM RN—the former Plymouth Naval Historian—I would still be researching the first dozen pages—I am indeed grateful for all his help. I must also record my thanks to the staff of the Imperial War Museum and Naval Historical branch for their help with photographs—and information. The mistakes are all my own work!

Looe
Cornwall

TRIBAL CLASS

Displacement (tons) 1,870 **Length** 377 ft. 6 ins. **Beam** 36 ft. 6 ins. **Draught** 9 ft. **Speed** 36½ knots **Armament** 6 x 4.7″ (3 twin mountings); 2 x 4″ A.A. (twin mounting); 7 smaller. **Torpedo Tubes** 4 x 21″ (quadruple mountings) **Complement** 190

SHIP	BUILDERS	LAUNCH DATE
ESKIMO	V. Armstrong, Tyne	3-9-1937

Notes
1946 Torpedo tubes removed and replaced by a deckhouse. Jan 1946 Accomodation Ship at Chatham. Then to Queensborough as Base Ship for B.Y.M.S. until late 1947. Feb 1948 in Reserve at Chatham. Aug 1949 arrived Troon to be broken up.

SHIP	BUILDERS	LAUNCH DATE
TARTAR	Swan Hunter, Wallsend	21-10-1937

Notes
Jan 1946 in Reserve at Devonport. Feb 1947 S.O.R.F. Devonport. 22 Feb 1948 arrived Newport to be broken up.

SHIP	BUILDERS	LAUNCH DATE
ASHANTI	Wm. Denny, Dumbarton	5-11-1937

Notes
Jan 1946 in Reserve at Rosyth. Feb 1947 in Reserve at Harwich. Feb 1948 Disposal list. July 1948 used in Ship Target Trails in Loch Striven. 12 April 1949 sold to Arnott Young, to be broken up at Troon.

SHIP	BUILDERS	LAUNCH DATE
NUBIAN	J.I. Thornycroft, Southampton	21-12-1937

Notes
1946-48 in Reserve at Portsmouth. 1949 used in Ship Target Trials. 25 June 1949 arrived Briton Ferry to be broken up.

HMS Eskimo (February 1939)

"J" CLASS

Displacement (tons) 1,690 Length 356 ft. 6 ins. Beam 35 ft. 9 ins. Draught 9 ft. Speed 36 knots Armament 6 x 4.7"; 4 x 40mm; 6 x 20mm Torpedo Tubes 10 x 21" (quintuple Mountings) Complement 220 (JERVIS 233)

SHIP	BUILDERS	LAUNCH DATE
JERVIS	Hawthorn Leslie, Hebburn	9-9-1938

Notes
14 May 1946 at Haifa. May 1947 in Reserve — Gareloch. 1948 used in Ship Target Trials. Sept 1949 broken up at Port Blannatyne.

SHIP	BUILDERS	LAUNCH DATE
JAVELIN	John Brown, Clydebank	21-12-1938

Notes
Jan 1946 14th Destroyer Flotilla in Mediterranean. 1946-48 in Reserve at Harwich. Then used in Ship Target Trials. 11 June 1949 sold to be broken up at Troon.

TOWN CLASS

Fifty Destroyers, which had been built during World War I, were transferred from the United States to the R.N. during September—November, 1940. They filled an important gap while the Emergency Construction Programme got under way. Known as the "Town Class" because nearly all of them were renamed after towns common to the U.S.A. and U.K. Exceptions were six ships transferred to the R.C.N., which were named after rivers common to U.S.A and U.K.

These ships were not active for long, but did fill a critical shortage.

In July 1944, six were transferred to Russia. Those ships that survived the war were afterwards soon placed in Reserve. By 1947 most had been scrapped. Two years later, those loaned to Russia were returned and also scrapped.

HMS Jarvis

HMS Javelin (June 1939)

'K' CLASS

Displacement (tons) 1,690 **Length** 356 ft. 6 ins. **Beam** 35 ft. 9 ins. **Draught** 9 ft. **Speed** 36 knots **Armament** 6 x 4.7"; 8 x 2 pdrs; 8 x 0.5"; 8 x 20mm (4 in KIMBERLEY) **Torpedo Tubes** 10 x 21" (2 x 5) **Complement** 183

SHIP	BUILDERS	LAUNCH DATE
KELVIN	Fairfield, Govan	19-1-1939

Notes
Jan 1946 in Reserve at Dartmouth. Feb 1947 in Reserve at Harwich. Feb 1948 Disposal list. 1949 Ship Target Trials. 6 April 1949 sold to be broken up at Troon.

SHIP	BUILDERS	LAUNCH DATE
KIMBERLEY	J.I. Thornycroft, Southampton	1-6-1939

Notes
Jan 1946 in Reserve at Dartmouth. Feb 1947 in Reserve at Harwich. Feb 1948 Disposal list. 1949 Ship Target Trials. Jun 1949 arrived Troon to be broken up.

'L' CLASS

HMS Loyal (November 1942)

Displacement (tons) 1,920 **Length** 362 ft. 6 ins. **Beam** 37 ft. **Draught** 10 ft. **Speed** 36½ knots **Armament** 6 x 4.7"; 1 x 3" A.A.; 4 x 2 pdr. A.A.; 2 x 20mm A.A.; 12 x 0.5" A.A. **Tropedo Tubes** 4 x 21" **Complement** 190

SHIP	BUILDERS	LAUNCH DATE
LOOKOUT	Scotts, Greenock	4-11-1940

Notes
Jan 1946-Feb 1948 in Reserve at Devonport. 29 Feb 1948 arrived Newport to be broken up.

SHIP	BUILDERS	LAUNCH DATE
LOYAL	Scotts, Greenock	8-10-1941

Notes
12 Oct 1944 became a constructive total loss. Feb 1947 in use as a Base Ship at Malta. Feb 1948 Disposal list at Malta. 5 Aug 1948 sold to be broken up at Milford Haven.

'M' CLASS

HMS Matchless (April 1946)

Displacement (tons) 1,920 **Length** 362 ft. 6 ins. **Beam** 36 ft. 9 ins. **Draught** 10 ft. **Speed** 33 knots **Armament** 6 x 4.7" (3 x 2); 4 x 2 pdrs; 8 x 0.5" A.A.; 2 x 20mm A.A. **Torpedo Tubes** 8 x 21" **Complement** 221

This class saw the introduction of gun turrets in destroyers.

SHIP	BUILDERS	LAUNCH DATE
MARNE	V. Armstrong, Tyne	30-10-1940

Notes
Jan 1946 paid off at Portsmouth. 1946-52 in Reserve at Portsmouth. 1952-57 in Reserve at Penarth. Aug 1957 sold to Turkey. Dec 1957-April 1959 refitted on the Tyne. 9 June 1959 handed over to Turkey (at Portsmouth). Renamed "MARESAL FEVSI CAKMAK". Aug 1971 Disposal list.

SHIP	BUILDERS	LAUNCH DATE
MATCHLESS	Alex Stephens, Linthouse	4-9-1941

Notes
1945-46 Mediterranean Fleet. 1946-52 in Reserve at Portsmouth. 1950-51 refitted at Woolston. 1952-57 in Reserve at Penarth. Aug 1957 sold to Turkey. Refitted at Govan. 16 July 1959 handed over to Turkey at Glasgow. Renamed "KILIC ALI PASHA". Aug 1971 Disposal list.

HMS Milne (July 1942)

SHIP	BUILDERS	LAUNCH DATE
METEOR	Alex Stephen, Linthouse	3-11-1941

Notes
1946-53 in Reserve at Devonport. 1951 refitted at Scotstoun. 1953-57 in Reserve at Penarth. Sept 1957 sold to Turkey. Refitted at Hebburn. 29 June 1959 handed over to Turkey at Portsmouth. Renamed "PIYALE PASHA". 1972 Disposal list.

SHIP	BUILDERS	LAUNCH DATE
MUSKETEER	Fairfield, Govan	2-12-1941

Notes
Jan 1946 paid off at Chatham. 1946-50 in Reserve at Harwich. 1950-51 refitted at Liverpool. 1951-54 in Reserve at Chatham. 1955 after refit at Belfast became Coastal Forces Depot and Living Ship at Harwich. Dec 1955 sold to be broken up at Sunderland.

SHIP	BUILDERS	LAUNCH DATE
MILNE	Scotts, Greenock.	30-12-1941

Completed by John Brown, Clydebank

Notes
1946-50 in Reserve at Harwich. 1947-48 Sea Cadet Training Ship. 1950 refitted at Rosyth. 1953-56 in Reserve at Penarth. 1957 Sold to Turkey. Refitted at Hull. 27 April 1959 handed over to Turkey, Renamed "ALP ARSLAM". Aug 1971 Disposal list.

'N' CLASS

HMS Nepal (June 1942)

Displacement (tons) 1,690 **Length** 356 ft. 6 ins. **Beam** 35 ft. 9 ins. **Draught** 9 ft. **Speed** 36 knots **Armament** 6 x 4.7" (twin mountings); 4 x 2 pdrs; 4 x 20mm; 8 x 0.5" **Torpedo Tubes** 10 x 21" (quintuple mountings) **Complement** 183

All were completed with a 4" A.A. gun in lieu of the after set of torpedo tubes, but the gun was later removed and the torpedo tubes fitted.

SHIP	BUILDERS	LAUNCH DATE
NOBLE (EX-NERISSA)	John Brown, Clydebank	7-5-1940

Notes
Served under the Polish Flag, as "PIORUN" from Oct 1940 to Sept 1946. Then returned to R.N. and renamed "NOBLE". 1946-52 in Reserve at Harwich. 1953 in Reserve at Chatham. 1954 in Reserve on the Tyne. Sept 1955 Disposal list. 2 Dec 1955 arrived Dunston to be broken up.

SHIP	BUILDERS	LAUNCH DATE
NAPIER	Fairfield, Govan	22-5-1940

Notes
Sept 1945 present at the Japanese Surrender in Tokyo Bay (R.A.N. crew). 25 Oct 1945 transferred back to the R.N. from R.A.N. — vice "QUALITY". 12 Dec 1945 paid off at Devonport. 1946-56 in Reserve Portsmouth/Devonport and Penarth. 17 Jan 1956 arrived Briton Ferry to be broken up.

SHIP	BUILDERS	LAUNCH DATE
NIZAM	John Brown, Clydebank	4-7-1940

Notes
13 Dec 1945 returned to Sheerness and to R.N. from R.A.N. 1946-53 in Reserve at Harwich. 1953-55 in Reserve at Chatham. 16 Nov 1955 arrived Grays, Essex to be broken up.

SHIP	BUILDERS	LAUNCH DATE
NORMAN	J.I. Thornycroft, Southampton	30-10-1940

Notes
12 Dec 1945 returned to Plymouth and to R.N. from R.A.N. 1946-49 in Reserve at Devonport. 1950 at Chatham. 1951-53 at Devonport. 1953-56 in Reserve at Penarth. 1 April 1958 arrived Newport to be broken up.

SHIP	BUILDERS	LAUNCH DATE
NEPAL (EX-NORSEMAN)	J.I. Thornycroft, Southampton	4-12-1941

Notes
Manned by the R.A.N. until 1945. 19 Nov 1945 sailed from Sydney for U.K., to rejoin R.N. 1 Jan 1946 at Rosyth, relieved WITCH as A/S Trials Ship, until 1949. 1950-53 in Reserve at Devonport. 1953-55 in Reserve at Penarth. 16 Jan 1956 arrived Briton Ferry to be broken up.

Transfers
NOBLE, built by Wm. Denny & Bros., Clydebank, launched 17 April 1941, was transferred to Royal Netherlands Navy in 1942 and renamed 'VAN GALEN''. Broken up in 1957. "NONPAREIL" transferred to Royal Netherlands Navy in 1942 and renamed "TJERK HIDDES". Broken up 1961.

"ONSLOW" CLASS
FIRST GROUP

Displacement (tons) 1,610 **Length** 345 ft. **Beam** 35 ft. **Draught** 9 ft. **Speed** 33 knots **Armament** 4 x 4.7"; 1 x 4" A.A.; 4 x 2 pdr; 4 x 20mm; 2 x .303 MG **Torpedo Tubes** 8 x 21" (quadruple mountings) **Complement** 176

SHIP	BUILDERS	LAUNCH DATE
ORIBI (EX-OBSERVER)	Fairfield, Govan	14-1-1941

Notes
Jan 1946 at Portsmouth pending transfer to Turkey as a replacement for "ITHURIEL". 18 June 1946 handed over to Turkey. Renamed "GAYRET". 1962 in use as Headquarters Ship. 1965 disposal list.

SHIP	BUILDERS	LAUNCH DATE
OFFA	Fairfield, Govan	11-3-1941

Notes
1946 Target Ship for submarines. Feb 1948 in Reserve at Devonport. April 1968 refitted at Devonport. 3 Nov 1949 transferred to Pakistan. Renamed "TARIG". 10 July 1959 returned to the R.N. at Portsmouth. 13 Oct 1959 arrived Sunderland to be broken up.

SHIP	BUILDERS	LAUNCH DATE
ONSLOW (EX-PAKENHAM)	John Brown, Clydebank	31-3-1941

Notes
Nov 1945 H.Q. Ship for operation "Deadlight" — moving U-Boats from Loch Ryan to scuttle off Bloody Foreland. 1946-47 in Reserve at Devonport. Aug 1947 Submarine Target Ship and A/S Equipment Trials Ship at Portsmouth. Oct 1947 paid off to reserve. 30 Sept 1949 Transferred (at Devonport) to Pakistan. Renamed "TIPPU SULTAN". 1954 refit at Malta. 1957-59 Type 16 conversion at Birkenhead. (Still in service in 1980).

HMS Oribi (May 1946)

SHIP	BUILDERS	LAUNCH DATE
ONSLAUGHT (EX-PATHFINDER)	Fairfield, Govan	9-10-1941

Notes

Jan 1946 became Submarine Tender at Portsmouth. 1947 Target Ship for 3rd Submarine Flotilla at Rothesay. 6 March 1951 transferred to Pakistan — renamed "TUGHRIL". 1957 Type 16 conversion at Liverpool. 1977 Disposal list.

"ONSLOW" CLASS
SECOND GROUP

Displacement (tons) 1,540 **Length** 345ft. **Beam** 35ft. **Draught** 9 ft. **Speed** 33 knots **Armament** 4 x 4"; 4 x 2 pdrs; 4 x 20mm; 2 x .303 MG **Torpedo Tubes** 8 x 21" (quadruple mountings) **Complement** 176

SHIP	BUILDERS	LAUNCH DATE
OPPORTUNE	J.I. Thornycroft, Southampton	21-1-1942

Notes

Jan 1946 Submarine Target Ship in Portsmouth Local Flotilla. 1947 Target for 3rd Submarine Flotilla at Rothesay; then 5th Submarine Flotilla at Portsmouth. 1949 refitted at Portsmouth. Feb 1950 Air Training Target Ship at Portsmouth. 1951-52 Nore Local Flotilla. Sept 1953 in Reserve at Portsmouth. 25 Nov 1955 arrived Milford Haven to be broken up.

SHIP	BUILDERS	LAUNCH DATE
OBDURATE	Wm. Denny, Dumbarton	19-2-1942

Notes

1946-47 Torpedo Training at Portsmouth. Feb 1948 Reserve at Portsmouth, then at Harwich. 1949-50 refit on the Tyne. 1950-52 Reserve at Chatham. 1952 refit at Birkenhead. 1953-56 Nore Local Squadron. 1957-59 Reserve at Portsmouth. April 1959 used in tests by N.C.R.E. at Rosyth. 30 Nov 1964 arrived Inverkeithing to be broken up.

HMS Onslaught (July 1946)

HMS Opportune (July 1946)

SHIP	BUILDERS	LAUNCH DATE
ORWELL	J.I. Thornycroft, Southampton	2-4-1942

Notes
1946-47 Portsmouth Local Flotilla — Torpedo training. 1947-49 Reserve at Harwich. 1949-50 refit at Cowes. 1950-52 Reserve at Chatham. 1952 converted to Type 16 Frigate at Rosyth Dockyard. Aug 1953 Submarine Target Ship for 3rd Submarine Flotilla, Rothesay. 1953-58 Devonport Local Squadron. Dec 1959 refit at Rosyth. 1960-61 Reserve at Rosyth. 1961-63 Reserve at Portsmouth. 28 June 1965 arrived Newport to be broken up.

SHIP	BUILDERS	LAUNCH DATE
OBEDIENT	Wm. Denny, Dumbarton	30-4-1942

Notes
Jan 1946 Portsmouth Local Flotilla — Torpedo training. Aug 1947 Reduced to Reserve at Sheerness. 1949 refit. 1950-57 Reserve at Chatham. 1957-62 Reserve at West Hartlepool. 19 Oct 1962 arrived Blyth to be broken up.

HMS Orwell (June 1947)

HMS Obedient (August 1946)

'P' CLASS

Displacement (tons) 1,550 **Length** 345 ft. **Beam** 35 ft. **Draught** 9 ft. **Speed** 33 knots **Armament** 4 x 4"; 4 x 2 pdr; 4 x 20mm (PORCUPINE 5 x 4"; 4 x 2 pdr; 2 x 20mm) **Torpedo Tubes** 8 x 21" (quadruple mountings) (PORCUPINE 4 x 21") **Complement** 176

SHIP	BUILDERS	LAUNCH DATE
PENN	V. Armstrong, Tyne	12-2-1941

Notes

Nov 1945 in East Indies as Air Target Ship. Sept 1946 British Pacific Fleet as Air Target Ship. Feb 1947 attached to 4th Submarine Flotilla in British Pacific Fleet. End of 1947 returned to U.K., where "A" gun mountings and torpedo tubes were removed. Feb 1948 reduced to Reserve at Harwich. April 1949 Ship Target Trials at Portland. July 1949 Damage Control Trials. 31 Jan 1950 arrived Troon to be broken up.

SHIP	BUILDERS	LAUNCH DATE
PETARD (EX-PERSISTENT)	V. Armstrong, Tyne	27-3-1941

Notes

Nov 1945-Sept 1945 6th Destroyer Flotilla, East Indies. Sept 1946-51 Harwich Reserve. 1951-53 Chatham Reserve. May 1953-Dec 1955 Type 16 conversion at Belfast. Jun 1956 at Southampton. Nov 1956-60 Devonport Reserve. Dec 1960 Plymouth Squadron. April 1961 Reduced to Reserve. 3 Sept 1961 commissioned at Portsmouth. June 1962 Reserve at Devonport. June 1967 arrived Bo'ness to be broken up.

HMS Petard (May 1945)

SHIP	BUILDERS	LAUNCH DATE
PATHFINDER (EX-ONSLAUGHT)	Hawthorn Leslie, Hebburn	10-4-1941

Notes
11 Feb 1945 badly damaged by Japanese aircraft at Ramree Island. Temporarily repaired (by R.E.M.E.) — Then to Colombo Dockyard. Sailed U.K. on starboard engine. June 1945 reduced to Reserve at Devonport. 1947-48 Ship Target Trials at Devonport. 17 Nov 1948 sold to Howells, Milford Haven.

SHIP	BUILDERS	LAUNCH DATE
PORCUPINE	V. Armstrong, Tyne	10-6-1941

Notes
Jan 1943 docked at Oran after torpedo damage, cut in half by French dockyard workmen. April 1943 towed to Gibraltar in two halves — "Pork" and "Pine". May 1943 towed to Portsmouth. April 1944 bow half in use as a Landing Craft base and then Minesweeper base. 5 May 1946 both halves sold. May 1947 broken up at Plymouth.

SHIP	BUILDERS	LAUNCH DATE
PALADIN	John Brown, Clydebank	11-6-1941

Notes
Nov 1945 Submarine Target Ship with 3rd Submarine Flotilla in Holy Loch. 1948-50 Harwich Reserve. 1951-52 Chatham Reserve. 1952-54 converted to Type 16 Frigate. March 1954 in Reserve. Jan 1958 commissioned from Reserve. March 1958 escort to "BRITANNIA" on Royal visit to Netherlands. 1959 Flagship of Admiral Commanding Reserves in Scottish Waters. April 1961 Reduced to Reserve. 25 Oct 1962 arrived Dunston to be broken up.

'Q' CLASS
Notes
QUIBERON, QUICKMATCH, QUALITY, QUADRANT and QUEENBOROUGH were all transferred to the R.A.N. by 1945. QUILLIAM was transferred to Royal Netherlands Navy in November, 1945.

HMS Paladin (June 1946)

"HUNT" CLASS DESTROYERS

These ships were originally designed for escort duties.
86 of the four classes were built—
23 Type 1's, 33 Type 2's, 28 Type 3's, 2 Type 4's
Most were later converted and classified as A.A. Frigates (as from June 1947).

TYPE 1 — "ATHERSTONE" TYPE

Displacement (tons) 1,000 **Length** 280 ft. **Beam** 29 ft. **Draught** 7 ft. 9 ins. **Speed** 27½ knots **Armament** 4 x 4″ A.A.; 2 x 20mm A.A. **Torpedo Tubes** none **Complement** 146

SHIP	BUILDERS	LAUNCH DATE
ATHERSTONE	Cammell Laird, Birkenhead	12-12-1939

Notes
25 Sept 1945 sailed from Mediterranean for Portsmouth and paid off into Reserve. 1953 laid up at Cardiff. 23 Nov 1957 sold to be broken up at Port Glasgow.

SHIP	BUILDERS	LAUNCH DATE
HAMBLEDON	Swan Hunter, Wallsend	12-12-1939

Notes
1945/6 Nore Destroyer Flotilla. May 1946 to Reserve at Harwich. Sept 1957 arrived on the Tyne to be broken up.

SHIP	BUILDERS	LAUNCH DATE
EGLINTON	V. Armstrong, Tyne	28-12-1939

Notes
May 1946 to Reserve at Hartlepool/Harwich/Hartlepool. 1951 refit at Hull. 24 June 1955 trials ship for Exercise 'Sleeping Beauty' designed to test state of reserve ships and time taken to bring them forward to active fleet. 28 May 1956 arrived Blyth to be broken up.

HMS Hambledon (November 1942)

SHIP	BUILDERS	LAUNCH DATE
FERNIE	John Brown, Clydebank	9-1-1940

Notes
1945-47 Air Target Ship (Rosyth). 1948 to Reserve at Chatham. 7 Nov 1956 arrived Port Glasgow to be broken up.

SHIP	BUILDERS	LAUNCH DATE
HOLDERNESS	Swan Hunter, Wallsend	8-2-1940

Notes
20 May 1946 to Reserve at Chatham. 20 Nov 1956 arrived Preston to be broken up.

SHIP	BUILDERS	LAUNCH DATE
PYTCHLEY	Scotts, Greenock	13-2-1940

Notes
Dec 1945 Aircraft Target Ship. 1946 Devonport Reserve. 1 Dec 1956 arrived Llanelly to be broken up.

SHIP	BUILDERS	LAUNCH DATE
GARTH	John Brown, Clydebank	14-2-1940

Notes
1945 Accommodation ship at Chatham—thence to Reserve. 25 Aug 1958 arrived Barrow to be broken up.

SHIP	BUILDERS	LAUNCH DATE
CATTISTOCK	Yarrow, Scotstoun	22-2-1940

Notes
Aug 1945 Portsmouth Command. March 1946 to Reserve at Devonport after repairs. Jan 1950 loan to R. Norwegian Navy considered but eventually cancelled. June 1957 arrived Newport to be broken up.

HMS Mendip (March 1948)

SHIP	BUILDERS	LAUNCH DATE
MENDIP	Swan Hunter, Wallsend	9-4-1940

Notes

20 May 1945 to Reserve at Harwich. May 1948 loaned to Chinese Navy; renamed "LIN FU". 1949 returned to R.N. at Hong Kong. 15 Nov 1949 sold to Egyptian Navy and renamed "MOHAMED — ALI EL-KEBIR". 1951 renamed "IBRAHIM EL AWAL". 31 Oct 1956 captured off Haifa by Israel. Renamed "HAIFA". 1972 withdrawn from service.

SHIP	BUILDERS	LAUNCH DATE
QUANTOCK	Scotts, Greenock	22-4-1940

Notes

1945 designated Air Target Training Ship—and placed in reserve. 16 Aug 1955 transferred at Portsmouth to Equadorian Navy; renamed "PRESIDENTE ALFARO", after being refitted by J. Samuel White, Cowes. 1978 Disposal list.

HMS Biencathra (August 1946)

SHIP	BUILDERS	LAUNCH DATE
CLEVELAND	Yarrow, Scotstoun	24-4-1940

Notes

25 Sept 1945 sailed from Gibraltar for Portsmouth and paid off into Reserve. 28 June 1957 wrecked near Swansea en route to be broken up at Llanelly. Wreck was stripped and blown up on 14 Dec 1959.

SHIP	BUILDERS	LAUNCH DATE
MEYNELL	Swan Hunter, Wallsend	7-6-1940

Notes

1947 Harwich Reserve. 18 Oct 1954 sold to Equardorian Navy and renamed "PRESIDENTE VELASCO IBARRA". 1978 disposal list.

SHIP	BUILDERS	LAUNCH DATE
SOUTHDOWN	J.S. White, Cowes	5-7-1940

Notes
1946 Aircraft Target Ship—thence Reserve. 1 Nov 1956 arrived Barrow to be broken up.

SHIP	BUILDERS	LAUNCH DATE
WHADDON	Alex Stephens, Govan	16-7-1940

Notes
29 Sept 1945 sailed from Gibraltar for Devonport and paid off into Reserve. 1959 broken up at Faslane.

SHIP	BUILDERS	LAUNCH DATE
COTSWOLD	Yarrow, Scotstoun	18-7-1940

Notes
June 1946 to Reserve at Portsmouth. 1948 at Harwich. 11 Sept 1957 arrived Grays to be broken up.

SHIP	BUILDERS	LAUNCH DATE
COTTESMORE	Yarrow, Scotstoun	5-9-1940

Notes
Aug 1945 to Reserve at Devonport. 17 Sept 1950 sold to Egypt (for £120,000 plus £83,000 for Naval & Armament Stores) renamed "IBRAHIM EL AWAL". 1951 renamed "MOHAMED ALI EL KEBIR". 1969 renamed "PORT SAID". (Still in service 1980).

HUNT CLASS —
TYPE 2 "BLANKNEY" TYPE

Displacement (tons) 1,050 **Length** 280 ft. **Beam** 31 ft. 6 ins. **Draught** 7 ft. 10 ins. **Speed** 27 knots **Armament** 6 x 4" A.A.; 1 x 2 pdr. Pom Pom; 2 x 20mm A.A. **Torpedo Tubes** none **Complement** 168

SHIP	BUILDERS	LAUNCH DATE
BLENCATHRA	Cammell Laird, Scotstoun	6-8-1940

Notes
Sept 1945-Dec 1947 Air Training Target Ship (Rosyth). 1948 to Reserve at Harwich—thence Barrow-in-Furness. 2 Jan 1957 arrived Barrow to be broken up.

SHIP	BUILDERS	LAUNCH DATE
LIDDESDALE	V. Armstrong, Tyne	19-8-1940

Notes
Dec 1945 to Reserve at Chatham. 1 Oct 1948 sold to J.J. King, Gateshead for breaking up.

SHIP	BUILDERS	LAUNCH DATE
BROCKLESBY	Cammell Laird, Birkenhead	30-9-1940

Notes
1945 sent to Wilhemshaven to 'show the flag' immediately after World War II—thence Aircraft Target Training Shp at Rosyth & Portsmouth. 1947 to Reserve at Portsmouth. 1951-2 Devonport Refit. 1952 2nd Frigate Squadron at Devonport—thence Portland. 1955 disarmed for service at Portland as Asdic Training & Trials Ship. 22 June 1963 arrived Portsmouth for last time to pay off after 22 years service. Oct 1968 arrived Faslane to be broken up.

HMS Brocklesby (December 1961)

SHIP	BUILDERS	LAUNCH DATE
FARNDALE	Swan Hunter, Wallsend	30-9-1940

Notes

Nov 1945 arrived Sheerness from Far East and placed in Reserve. 1946-47 Nore Flotilla—thence Reserve. 4 Dec 1962 arrived Blyth for breaking up.

SHIP	BUILDERS	LAUNCH DATE
AVON VALE	John Brown, Clydebank	23-10-1940

Notes

1945 Mediterranean. 1946 Devonport Reserve. 15 May 1958 arrived Sunderland to be broken up.

SHIP	BUILDERS	LAUNCH DATE
SILVERTON	J.S. White, Cowes	4-12-1940

Notes

1945 Mediterranean. 1946 Devonport Reserve. 1941-46 with Polish Navy as "KRAKOWIAK". Sept 1946 to Reserve at Harwich. 29 Sept 1956 arrived Milford Haven to be broken up.

SHIP	BUILDERS	LAUNCH DATE
LAMERTON	Swan Hunter, Wallsend	14-12-1940

Notes

Dec 1945 returned to UK from refit at Simonstown. 20 March 1946 paid off at Harwich. 27 Oct 1952 lent to Indian Navy for 3 years; named "GOMATI", but loan extended. 1975 disposal list.

SHIP	BUILDERS	LAUNCH DATE
BLANKNEY	John Brown, Clydebank	19-12-1940

Notes

10 Dec 1945 sailed from Cape Town after local refit—thence to reserve at Devonport. March 1959 arrived Blyth to be broken up.

HMS Farndale (June 1943)

SHIP	BUILDERS	LAUNCH DATE
CROOME	Alex Stephen, Govan	30-1-1941

Notes

Oct 1945 returned to Devonport from Mediterranean—and paid off into Reserve. 13 Aug 1957 arrived Briton Ferry to be broken up.

SHIP	BUILDERS	LAUNCH DATE
CHIDDINGFOLD	Scotts, Greenock	10-3-1941

Notes

16 Nov 1945 returned to Portsmouth from East Indies—and paid off into Reserve. 1950-52 laid up at Harwich. July 1952 towed to Liverpool for refit. 27 Oct 1952 lent to Indian Navy for 3 years; named "GANGA"; but loan extended. 1975 disposal list.

SHIP	BUILDERS	LAUNCH DATE
EXMOOR	Swan Hunter, Wallsend	12-3-1941

Notes

Sept 1945 returned to Portsmouth from Toranto refit—thence to Reserve. 1953 loaned to Denmark and renamed "VALDEMAR SEJR". 1966 sold to be broken up.

SHIP	BUILDERS	LAUNCH DATE
BADSWORTH	Cammell Laird, Birkenhead	17-3-1941

Notes

1946 purchased by Royal Norwegian Navy and renamed "ARENDAL" used as Cadets' Training Ship. 1961 broken up.

SHIP	BUILDERS	LAUNCH DATE
CALPE	Swan Hunter, Wallsend	28-4-1941

Notes
Nov 1945 returned to Chatham from Far East—and paid off into Reserve. 1952 loaned to Denmark and renamed "ROLF KRAKE". 1966 sold.

SHIP	BUILDERS	LAUNCH DATE
MIDDLETON	V.Armstrong Tyne	12-5-1941

Notes
Aug-Dec 1945 Simonstown Refit. Jan 1946 returned to Portsmouth—and paid off into Reserve. 4 Oct 1957 arrived Blyth to be broken up.

SHIP	BUILDERS	LAUNCH DATE
WHEATLAND	Yarrow Scotstoun	7-6-1941

Notes
1945 to Reserve at Devonport. Sept 1953 towed to Gibraltar for local reserve. Aug 1955 towed back to Harwich for service—as a hulk—as an artificial harbour. 20 Sept 1959 arrived Bo'ness to be broken up.

SHIP	BUILDERS	LAUNCH DATE
BEAUFORT	Cammell Laird, Birkenhead	9-6-1941

Notes
10 June 1945 arrived Cardiff from Mediterranean for refit but later abandoned and towed to Devonport and Reserve. 1952 loaned to Royal Norwegian Navy, renamed "HAUGESUND". 1965 disposal list.

SHIP	BUILDERS	LAUNCH DATE
COWDRAY	Scotts, Greenock	22-7-1941

Notes
5 Dec 1945 arrived Chatham from Far East. 1946-9 Nore Destroyer Flotilla (Aug 1947 Sheerness Refit). Jan 1950 to Reserve. 3 Sept 1959 arrived Gateshead to be broken up.

SHIP	BUILDERS	LAUNCH DATE
BEDALE	Hawthorn Leslie, Hebburn	23-7-1941

Notes
Sept 1945 to Reserve at Harwich after sevice with Polish Navy (as SLAVAK.) 27 Oct 1952 lent to Indian Navy for 3 years as "GODAVAR" but loan extended. 1979 Disposal list.

SHIP	BUILDERS	LAUNCH DATE
LAUDERDALE	J.I. Thornycroft, Southampton	5-8-1941

Notes
7 Dec 1946 completed refit at Durban and transferred to Royal Hellenic Navy as "AIGAION". 1960 broken up in Greece.

SHIP	BUILDERS	LAUNCH DATE
TETCOTT	J.S. White, Cowes	12-8-1941

Notes
16 Oct 1945 sailed from Gibraltar refit for Portsmouth—and Reserve. Sept 1947 Sheerness Refit—thence Reserve. 24 September 1956 arrived Milford Haven to be broken up.

HMS Cowdray (October 1948)

HMS Bicester (March 1949)

SHIP	BUILDERS	LAUNCH DATE
BICESTER	Hawthorn Leslie, Hebburn	5-9-1941

Notes
4 Dec 1945 returned to UK from Indian Ocean. 1946—joined Nore Destroyer Flotilla—served as Leader until Jan 1950—thence to Reserve. 22 Aug 1956 arrived Grays to be broken up.

SHIP	BUILDERS	LAUNCH DATE
LEDBURY	J.I. Thornycroft, Southampton	27-9-1941

Notes
14 Dec 1945 arrived Portsmouth after Gibraltar refit. March 1946 to Reserve at Portsmouth. 1958 broken up at Rosyth.

SHIP	BUILDERS	LAUNCH DATE
WILTON	Yarrow, Scotstoun	17-10-1941

Notes
Aug 1945-Jan 1946—Simonstown Refit. 10 Feb 1946 arrived Devonport and paid off into Reserve. Dec 1949 re-commissioned for 4th Training Flotilla (Rosyth). 1952 reduced to Reserve—thence HQ Ship South Wales Reserve Fleet. 30 Nov 1959 arrived Faslane to be broken up.

SHIP	BUILDERS	LAUNCH DATE
BLACKMORE	Alex Stephen, Govan	2-12-1941

Notes
8 Oct 1945 sailed from Singapore for Devonport—thence to Reserve. 1952 loaned to Denmark as "ESBERN SNARE". 1966 broken up.

HMS Oakley (October 1958)

SHIP	BUILDERS	LAUNCH DATE
OAKLEY	Yarrow, Scotstoun	15-1-1942

Notes

Oct 1945 returned to Portsmouth from Mediterranean. Dec 1945 to Reserve at Portsmouth. 1958 transferred to West German Navy renamed "GNEISENAU". 1972 broken up.

SHIP	BUILDERS	LAUNCH DATE
ZETLAND	Yarrow, Scotstoun	7-3-1942

Notes

June-Oct 1945 Alexandria Refit—thence to UK. 20 Apr 1946 paid off into Reserve and assigned to Solent Division R.N.V.R. as Drillship. 2 Sept 1954 lent to Norway and renamed "TROMSO". 1965 broken up by Sarpsborg Shipbreakers.

HUNT CLASS — TYPE 3

Displacement (tons) 1,050 Length 280 ft. Beam 31ft. 6 ins.
Draught 7ft. 10ins. Speed 27 knots Armament 4 x 4" A.A.; 4 x 2
pdr. Pom-Pom; 2 x 20 or 40mm A.A. Torpedo Tubes 2 x 21"
Complement 168

SHIP	BUILDERS	LAUNCH DATE
BLEASDALE	V. Armstrong, Tyne	23-7-1941

Notes
16 Nov 1945 to Reserve at Chatham. Feb 1946 recommissioned for Nore local Flotilla.
18 Apr 1947 Operation 'Big Bang'—the 'instant demilitarisation' of Heligoland.
Acted as firing ship for radio initiated demolition charges. 21 Apr 1952 to Reserve at
Sheerness. Late 1952 Portsmouth refit—thence Reserve. 14 Sept 1956 arrived Blyth to
be broken up.

SHIP	BUILDERS	LAUNCH DATE
ALBRIGHTON	John Brown, Clydebank	11-10-1941

Notes
Dec 1945 completed Immingham Refit—thence to Reserve at Devonport. Nov 1957
sold to West Germany and renamed "RAULE" (on 9 April 1959). 1969 broken up.

SHIP	BUILDERS	LAUNCH DATE
BELVIOR	Cammell Laird, Birkenhead	18-11-1941

Notes
1945-46 Portsmouth Local Flotilla. Loan to France not agreed. Reduced to Reserve 29
May 1946. June 1953 Portsmouth Refit. 21 Oct 1957 arrived Bo'ness to be broken up.

HMS Bleasdale (September 1950)

HMS Belvoir (February 1946)

SHIP	BUILDERS	LAUNCH DATE
CATTERICK	V. Armstrong, Barrow	22-11-1941

Notes
7 Dec 1946 completed refit at Durban and transferred to Royal Hellenic Navy—renamed "HASTINGS". 1963 broken up in Greece.

SHIP	BUILDERS	LAUNCH DATE
GLAISDALE	Cammell Laird, Birkenhead	5-1-1942

Notes
1946 transferred to Royal Norwegian Navy and renamed "NARVIK". 1961 broken up in Denmark.

SHIP	BUILDERS	LAUNCH DATE
MELBREAK	Swan Hunter, Wallsend	5-3-1942

Notes
7 May 1945 considerable damage on grounding, repaired at Sheerness—thence to Reserve at Chatham. 22 Nov 1956 arrived Grays to be broken up.

SHIP	BUILDERS	LAUNCH DATE
HAYDON	V. Armstrong, Tyne	2-4-1942

Notes
1945-47 3rd Destroyer Flotilla Mediterranean—Palestinian Patrols. 1952 laid up at West Hartlepool. 18 May 1958 arrived Dunston to be broken up.

HMS Melbreak (June 1953)

SHIP	BUILDERS	LAUNCH DATE
TANATSIDE	Yarrow, Scotstoun	30-4-1942

Notes
Dec 1945 reduced to "Care & Maintenance Only" at Malta. 1946 transferred to Royal Hellenic Navy and renamed "ADRIAS". 1964 Broken up.

SHIP	BUILDERS	LAUNCH DATE
WENSLEYDALE	Yarrow, Scotstoun	20-6-1942

Notes
March 1946 laid up at West Hartlepool. Feb 1947 arrived Blyth to be broken up.

43

SHIP	BUILDERS	LAUNCH DATE
EASTON	J.S. White, Cowes	11-7-1942

Notes

1945-47 Portsmouth Local Flotilla and 3rd Escort Flotilla (Portland). 1949-52 laid up at Rosyth for disposal but used as training ship for apprentices. Jan 1953 broken up at Rosyth.

SHIP	BUILDERS	LAUNCH DATE
EGGESFORD	J.S. White, Cowes	12-9-1942

Notes

1945 Basic A/S Training Flotilla (Cambletown)—thence Portland. 1946 to Reserve. 1952 laid up at Penarth. 1958 transferred to West Germany and renamed "BROMMY". 1969 broken up.

SHIP	BUILDERS	LAUNCH DATE
STEVENSTONE	J.S. White, Cowes	23-11-1942

Notes

1946-47 3rd Destroyer Flotilla in Mediterranean. 1948 Chatham repairs. 2 Sept 1959 arrived Dunston to be broken up.

SHIP	BUILDERS	LAUNCH DATE
TALYBONT	J.S. White, Cowes	3-2-1943

Notes

1945 Malta refit—thence 3rd Destroyer Flotilla Mediterranean. 1946-47 Palestinian Patrols—thence to Reserve. 7 Nov 1956 towed from West Hartlepool to Rosyth for use as Harbour Training Ship (attached to CALEDONIA). 1960 relieved by CHEVIOT. 10 March 1961 arrived Charlestown to be broken up.

HMS Easton (June 1947)

HUNT CLASS — TYPE 4

HMS Brissenden (Feb 1943)

Displacement (tons) 1,175 **Length** 296 ft. **Beam** 33ft. 4 ins.
Draught 8 ft. **Speed** 25 knots **Armament** 6 x 4″ A.A.; 4 x 2 pdrs;
6 to 8x 20mm A.A. **Torpedo Tubes** 3 x 21″ **Complement** 170
Both ships fitted out for Arctic service by builders.

SHIP	BUILDERS	LAUNCH DATE
BRECON	J.I. Thornycroft, Southampton	27-6-1942

Notes
26 Aug 1945 arrived Colombo from Mediterranean to join East Indies Fleet. 3 Nov 1945 sailed from Far East for Portsmouth and Reserve. 1946-62 in Reserve. 17 Sept 1962 arrived Faslane to be broken up.

SHIP	BUILDERS	LAUNCH DATE
BRISSENDEN	J.I. Thornycroft, Southampton	15-9-1942

Notes
1945-47 3rd Destroyer Flotilla Mediterranean—Palestinian Patrol. Malta Refit. 6 Nov 1947 ordered back to UK—and Reserve. 1948-57 Category A Reserve. 1959 placed on Sales List and laid up at Lisahally. 3 March 1965 arrived Dalmuir to be broken up.

EX-GERMAN DESTROYER

HMS Nonsuch (October 1948)

Displacement (tons) 2,650 Length 403 ft. 6 ins. Beam 38 ft. 4 ins. Draught 9 ft. 6 ins. Speed 36 knots Armament 5 x 5.9"; 6 x 37mm A.A.; 16 x 20mm A.A. Torpedo Tubes 8 x 21" Complement 285

SHIP	BUILDERS	LAUNCH DATE
NONSUCH (EX-Z38)	Germania Werft, Kiel	11-11-1941

Notes

This was the only ex-German destroyer commissioned by the R.N. Broken up May 1950. Used to test high pressure boilers used by the Germans.

DESTROYERS — OR FRIGATES?

Advances in anti-submarine warfare and the increased performance of submarines led to a programme in the early 1950s to update the capabilities of certain destroyer classes by alterations to the armament and the fitting of improved sonar.

Consideration was given to the conversion of the available fast hulls of the M to Z-class. but as the programme proceeded the number of ships scheduled for conversion was reduced and many were then placed on the sales list.

As these ships started life as destroyers they are included in this book.

The conversions were of two types:

Type 15 (Full): The ship was stripped of all upperworks to leave the basic hull and funnel. The shell plating was extended aft from the break of the focsle to provide a complete new enclosed deck. An enclosed bridge was fitted at the former 'A' gun mounting position. A twin 40mm mounting was fitted abaft the bridge, two short lattice masts were stepped and aft of the mainmast a twin 4″ mounting and director were installed. Further aft, two anti-submarine mortars (Limbo) were fitted together with associated projectile handling rooms. Provision was also made to ship torpedo tubes on the upper deck (8 single fixed and two twin trainable) but few ships were ever fitted.

Three ships (TROUBRIDGE, ULSTER and ZEST) were completed with 'Leopard' (frigate) type enclosed bridges fitted one deck higher and with the twin 40mm mounted immediately forward.

Type 16 (Limited): This conversion was much simpler than that of the Type 15. The existing armament was removed and replaced by a twin 4″ at 'B' mounting. A set of torpedo tubes on the after site and several 40mm (the 'T' class included a twin 40mm) were added. Structural alterations were limited to the building of a mortar-bomb handling room at 'X' mounting with two squids mountings fitted immediately forward.

TEAZER, TUMULT and TERPSICHORE were fitted with a small enclosed bridge.

Before . . . HMS Roebuck (July 1943)

After . . . HMS Roebuck (July 1960)

'R' CLASS

Displacement (tons) 1,705 (ROTHERHAM 1,750 tons) **Length** 358 ft. 9 ins. **Beam** 35 ft. 9 ins. **Draught** 9ft. 6 ins. **Speed** 36½ knots **Armament** 4 x 4.7"; 4 x 2 pdr. Pom-Poms; 8 x 20mm A.A. ("RAIDER" had 4 x 40mm A.A. in place of 2 pdrs.) **Torpedo Tubes** 8 x 21" **Complement** 175.

SHIP	BUILDERS	LAUNCH DATE
ROTHERHAM	John Brown, Clydebank	21-3-1942

Notes

Jan 1946 Portsmouth Reserve. Oct 1947 at Portland. Aug 1948 refit at Portsmouth prior to transfer to Royal Indian Navy. Handed over 29 July 1949 — and renamed "RAJPUT". 1976 Disposal list.

SHIP	BUILDERS	LAUNCH DATE
RAIDER	Cammel Laird, Birkenhead	1-4-1942

Notes

Jan 1946 Devonport Reserve. 6 May 1946 commissioned as tender to aircraft carriers in the Mediterranean until Aug 1947. Oct 1947-1948 Devonport Reserve. Sept 1949 transferred to R.I.N. — renamed "RANA". 1976 Disposal list.

SHIP	BUILDERS	LAUNCH DATE
REDOUBT	John Brown, Clydebank	2-5-1942

Notes

Jan 1946-47 Chatham Reserve. August 1947 Harwich Reserve. 1948-49 refit at Chatham prior to transfer to Royal Indian Navy. 4 July 1949 handed over to R.I.N. — renamed "RANJIT". 1979 Disposal list.

HMS Rotherham (August 1946)

SHIP	BUILDERS	LAUNCH DATE
RACEHORSE	John Brown, Clydebank	1-6-1942

Notes
Jan 1946 Portsmouth Reserve. 1948 in use as target ship. May 1949 in the Gareloch. Oct 1949 Ship Target Trials. Feb 1950 arrived Troon to be broken up.

SHIP	BUILDERS	LAUNCH DATE
RELENTLESS	John Brown, Clydebank	15-7-1942

Notes
Jan 1946-47 Chatham Reserve. August 1947-49 Harwich Reserve. 1949-51 conversion to Type 15 Frigate at Portsmouth Dockyard. 27 Oct 1954 badly damaged in collison with "VIGILANT". Oct 1956 Reserve in Gareloch. June 1957-60 Chatham Reserve. 1960-64 Rosyth Reserve. 27 June 1964 commissioned for 29th Escort Squadron to replace "DIANA". Dec 1964 transferred to 26th ES. August 1965 Disposal list. 1971 Broken up at Inverkeithing.

SHIP	BUILDERS	LAUNCH DATE
RAPID	Cammell Laird, Birkenhead	16-7-1942

Notes
11 April 1946 commissioned as Air Training Target Ship and Attendendant Destroyer to Aircraft Carriers. Feb 1947 based at Rosyth. June 1951-Oct 1953 converted to Type 15 Frigate by Alex Stephen — Clyde. October 1953 at Portland/Portsmouth for trials. 1 June 1954-1965 Portsmouth Reserve. 1965 disposal list. 13 Dec 1966 left Portsmouth for Rosyth to refit as Sea Going Tender to "CALEDONIA". May 1967 commissioned. 1976 damaged whilst in service as a target for missiles launched from "BRISTOL". Docked at Devonport for repairs. 1977 Target Ship at Milford Haven. 1978 Returned to Disposal list. 1981 sunk by 2 torpedoes from HMS ONYX in Western Approaches.

HMS Rapid (February 1947)

SHIP	BUILDERS	LAUNCH DATE
ROCKET	Scotts, Greenock	28-10-1942

Notes

Jan 1946 at Chatham. 1946-48 Air Target Ship at Rosyth. May 1949 Portsmouth Reserve. July 1949-51 converted to Type 15 Frigate at Devonport Dockyard. 18 May 1951 commissioned for 3rd Training Squadron (Londonderry). Sept 1954 Rosyth Reserve. 1955 commissioned at Chatham. Nov 1956 Chatham Reserve. Dec 1957 Portsmouth Reserve. 28 Oct 1960 commissioned at Portsmouth. 26 Nov 1960 sailed to Far East to join 6th Frigate Squadron. 11 May 1962 Portsmouth — to Reserve. 14 March 1967 towed from Portsmouth for breaking up at Dalmuir.

SHIP	BUILDERS	LAUNCH DATE
ROEBUCK	Scotts, Greenock	10-12-1942

Notes

Jan 1946 C. & M. at Devonport. June 1949 escorted "DUKE OF YORK" during Royal visit to Channel Islands. 1951-53 converted to Type 15 Frigate at Devonport Dockyard. October 1953-56 5th FS in Mediterranean. July 1956 Devonport Reserve. 1957 refitted at Devonport as Training Ship. Nov 1957 replaced "CARRON" in Dartmouth Training Squadron. 1959-60 refit. May 1960 commissioned for 17th ES. Oct 1962 Devonport Reserve. 1968 used at Rosyth in underwater explosion trials. 8 August 1968 arrived Inverkeithing to be broken up. (Photo see page 49).

HMS Rocket (September 1947)

'S' CLASS

Displacement (tons) 1,710 (SAUMAREZ 1,730 tons) **Length** 362 ft. 9 ins. **Beam** 35 ft. 9 ins. **Draught** 10 ft. **Speed** 36¾ knots **Armament** SAVAGE 4 x 4.5"; 12 x 20mm A.A. SAUMAREZ 4 x 4.7"; 2 x 40mm; 8 x 20mm A.A.; **Torpedo Tubes** 8 x 21" (quadruple mountings) **Complement** 180 (SAUMAREZ 225)

SHIP	BUILDERS	LAUNCH DATE
SAVAGE	Hawthorn Leslie, Hebburn	24-9-1942

Notes
Sept 1945-April 1947 Gunnery Firing Ship at Portsmouth. Feb 1948-1950 Chatham Reserve. 5 July 1950 commissioned at Chatham for experiments with shafts and propellors. 1952 refit at Chatham. July 1954 Chatham modernisation. Nov 1956 Chatham Reserve. Dec 1957 Portsmouth Reserve. 1960 Disposal list. 11 April 1962 arrived Newport to be broken up.

SHIP	BUILDERS	LAUNCH DATE
SAUMAREZ	Hawthorn Leslie, Hebburn	20-11-1942

Notes
1946 3rd DF in Mediterranean. 22 Oct 1946 with "VOLAGE" was mined in Corfu Channel. 1947 at Malta. Feb 1948 approved to scrap. 23 August 1950 hulk arrived Gibraltar in tow of "SALVEDA". 8 Sept 1950 sold. Oct 1950 arrived Charlestown to be broken up.

HMS Savage (February 1946)

'T' CLASS

Displacement (tons) 1,710 (TROUBRIDGE 1,730 tons) **Length** 362 ft. 9 ins. **Beam** 35 ft. 9 ins. **Draught** 10 ft. **Speed** 36 knots **Armament** 4 x 4.7″; 4 x 2 pdr Pom-Poms; 4 x 20mm A.A. (TUSCAN 4 x 4.7″; 7 x 40mm A.A.) (TEAZER only 3 x 4.7″) **Torpedo Tubes** 8 x 21″ (quadruple mountings)(TUMULT 6 x 21″ (1 x 4, 2 x 1)) **Complement** 180

SHIP	BUILDERS	LAUNCH DATE
TUSCAN	Swan Hunter, Wallsend	28-5-1942

Notes
1946-52 Portsmouth Reserve. 1949-50 refit at Cammell Laird, Birkenhead. May 1952-Sept 1953 converted to Type 16 Frigate by Mount Stuart Dry Docks, Cardiff. October 1953 Devonport Reserve. 1954 Portsmouth Reserve. 1960 Chatham Reserve 1961-63 Portsmouth Operational Reserve. 26 May 1966 arrived Bo'ness to to be broken up.

SHIP	BUILDERS	LAUNCH DATE
TYRIAN	Swan Hunter, Wallsend	27-7-1942

Notes
1946-51 Harwich/Sheerness/Harwich Reserve. 1951-52 converted to Type 16 Frigate by Harland & Wolff, Liverpool. August 1952-56 2nd Training Squadron, at Portland. Nov 1956 Chatham Reserve. 1957-65 Lisahally Reserve. 9 March 1965 arrived Troon to be broken up.

HMS Tuscan (April 1946)

SHIP	BUILDERS	LAUNCH DATE
TROUBRIDGE	John Brown, Clydebank	23-9-1942

Notes
Dec 1946-August 1949 replaced "SUMAREZ" as leader of 3rd DF in Mediterranean. 16 Aug 1949. Returned to Chatham and Reserve. 1955-57 converted to Type 15 Frigate by Portsmouth Dockyard (completed by J. White, Cowes). Dec 1957 8th FS on America and West Indies Station. 1960 8th FS Home Fleet. Feb 1962 West Indies. 15 May 1963 towed from Portsmouth to Malta for refit. 7 Sept 1964 commissioned for 27th Escort Squadron. 27 March 1969 paid off at Chatham. 5 May 1970 arrived Newport to be broken up.

SHIP	BUILDERS	LAUNCH DATE
TUMULT	John Brown, Clydebank,	9-11-1942

Notes
1946 Portsmouth Reserve. 1953-54 converted to Type 16 Frigate by Grayson Rollo, Birkenhead. Nov 1956 2nd Training Squadron at Portsmouth. Dec 1957-Dec 1960 Chatham Reserve. Dec 1960-Oct 1965 Rosyth Reserve. 25 Oct 1965 arrived Dalmuir to be broken up.

SHIP	BUILDERS	LAUNCH DATE
TEAZER	Cammell Laird, Birkenhead	7-1-1943

Notes
1946-53 Devonport Reserve. 1953-54 converted to Type 16 Frigate by Mountstuart Dry Docks, Cardiff. Jan 1959 replaced "Grenville" in 2nd TS. Sept 1961 Disposal list. 7 August 1965 arrived Dalmuir to be broken up.

HMS Tumult (March 1946)

HMS Troubridge (March 1943)

HMS Troubridge (January 1969)

HMS Termagant (October 1954)

SHIP	BUILDERS	LAUNCH DATE
TERMAGANT	Wm. Denny Dumbarton	22-3-1943

Notes
1946-51 Portsmouth Reserve. 1952-53 converted to Type 16 Frigate by Grayson and Rollo, Birkenhead. 16 May 1953 completed trials and joined 3rd Submarine Flotilla, at Rothesay, as Target Ship. Aug 1957 Devonport Reserve. Oct 1958 commissioned for trials. 1960-65 Lisahally Reserve. 5 Nov 1965 arrived Dalmuir to be broken up.

SHIP	BUILDERS	LAUNCH DATE
TENACIOUS	Cammell Laird, Birkenhead	24-3-1943

Notes
1946-49 Devonport Reserve. 23 Jan 1949 arrived in Mersey for refit. Nov 1949 Commissioned as Target Ship for 3rd Submarine Flotilla, at Rothsay. Jan 1951-52 converted to Type 16 Frigate at Rosyth. Aug 1954 Rosyth Reserve. Nov 1956 Barrow Reserve. Sept 1963 towed to Plymouth. 29 June 1965 arrived Troon to be broken up.

SHIP	BUILDERS	LAUNCH DATE
TERPSICHORE	Wm. Denny, Dumbarton	17-6-1943

Notes
1946-53 Devonport Reserve. 1953-54 converted to Type 16 Frigate by Thornycroft, Woolston. 1955 Devonport Reserve. Dec 1957 refit at Devonport. 1960-66 Lisahally Reserve. 17 May 1966 arrived Troon to be broken up.

HMS Tenacious (December 1952)

HMS Terpsichore (1954)

"U" CLASS

Displacement (tons) 1,710 (GRENVILLE 1,730 tons) **Lenght** 362 ft. 9 ins. **Beam** 35 ft. 9 ins. **Draught** 10 ft. **Speed** 36 knots **Armament** 4 x 4.7"; 4 x 2 pdr. Pom Poms; 4 x 20mm A.A. **Torpedo Tubes** 8 x 21" (quadruple mountings) **Complement** 180

SHIP	BUILDERS	LAUNCH DATE
GRENVILLE	Swan Hunter, Wallsend	12-10-1942

Notes

1946 25th Destroyer Flotilla in British Pacific Fleet. 1946 Portsmouth/Harwich Reserve. 1951 Plymouth Local Flotilla. 1 Oct 1951 collided with Italian "ALEGO" off Start Point. Holed. 3 men were killed, 4 missing, 1 injured. 5 Aug 1952 Commissioned after repairs at Devonport. 1953-54 converted to Type 15 Frigate. 10 March 1954 commissioned as Leader of 2nd Training Squadron, Portland. 1957 helicopter landing pad fitted aft for trials. Dec 1958 replaced "TORQUAY" in 5th FS. 1960-64 Gibraltar Reserve. June 1966 arrived Portsmouth in tow from Gibraltar. March 1967 Portsmouth — Trials and Reserve. April 1969 Portsmouth refitting as A.S.W.E. Trials Ship. Oct 1969 replaced "WAKEFUL" in 2nd FS. 1970 Fitted with Scot Satellite Terminal for trials. 1974 Sales list. 1982 at Portsmouth pending disposal.

SHIP	BUILDERS	LAUNCH DATE
ULSTER	Swan Hunter, Wallsend	9-11-1942

Notes

Oct 1945-Feb 1946 under repair at Chatham. 1946-50 Boys Training at Rosyth. 27 May 1950 Dartmouth Training Squadron. Jan 1951-Dec 1952 Plymouth Local Flotilla. Dec 1952-54 Devonport Reserve. 1954-56 converted, at Chatham, to Type 15 Frigate. 7 March 1957 commissioned for 8th FS. Sept 1963 paid off to C. & M. at Devonport. Feb 1964-May 1965 refit at Devonport. 15 July 1965 commissioned for 2nd FS. Sept 1966 30 foot section of stern replaced by similar section cut from "URCHIN". 1967 Navigation Training Ship for "DRYAD". 1977 towed to Plymouth for use as Harbour Training Ship for "RALEIGH" new entries. 29 Oct 1980 left Plymouth in tow for Inverkeithing to be broken up.

HMS Grenville (April 1946)

HMS Ulster (July 1950)

D83

SHIP	BUILDERS	LAUNCH DATE
URCHIN	V. Armstrong, Barrow	8-3-1943

Notes
1947-48 Harwich Reserve. 1948-Jan 1952 Chatham Reserve. 1952-54 converted to Type 15 Frigate by Barclay Curle on the Clyde. 3 June 1954 commissioned for 3rd TS, Londonderry. Nov 1956 Portsmouth/Devonport Reserve. Dec 1957 refitted as Training frigate. Aug 1959 commissioned for Dartmouth Training Squadron. 1964 at Devonport, paid off to Reserve. 1966 stern cut away and fitted to "ULSTER". 6 Aug 1967 arrived Troon to be broken up.

SHIP	BUILDERS	LAUNCH DATE
ULYSSES	Cammell Laird, Birkenhead	22-4-1943

Notes
1946-51 Devonport Reserve. Dec 1951 commissioned for Plymouth Local Flotilla. 1953 Devonport Reserve. 1954-55 converted to Type 15 Frigate at Devonport. 18 Oct 1955 Commissioned for 6th FS in Mediterranean/Home Fleet. April 1958 operation "Grapple" — nuclear tests, Christmas Island. 27 Oct 1958 collided with "UNDINE" off Ushant. 1960 Training Ship, Plymouth Local Squadron. Dec 1960 Devonport Reserve. 1969 broken up at Plymouth.

SHIP	BUILDERS	LAUNCH DATE
URANIA	V. Armstrong, Barrow	19-5-1943

Notes
1947-50 Devonport Reserve. 11 Nov 1950 arrived Tyne for refit by Hawthorn Leslie. 1952 Harwich Reserve. 23 April 1953 arrived Liverpool for conversion to Type 15 Frigate by Harland & Wolff. 2 Jan 1955 Commissioned for 6th FS in Mediterranean. 1958 Devonport Reserve then refit. 7 Jan 1959 commissioned for trials, then to Reserve. May-Sept 1962 Refit at Rosyth. 1962-Jan 1967 Devonport Reserve. Jan 1967 transferred to Operational Reserve, Portsmouth. 2 Feb 1971 arrived Faslane to be broken up.

HMS Urchin (July 1963)

HMS Ulysses (April 1951)

SHIP	BUILDERS	LAUNCH DATE
UNDINE	J.I. Thorneycroft, Southampton	1-6-1943

Notes
May 1946 returned to U.K., and Reserve at Harwich. May 1949 refit at Chatham. 1950-52 Sheerness Reserve. 1952 converted to Type 15 Frigate on the Clyde. 1954-60 6th FS in Mediterranean. 1960-65 Portsmouth Reserve. 12 Nov 1965 left Portsmouth for Newport to be broken up.

SHIP	BUILDERS	LAUNCH DATE
UNDAUNTED	Cammell Laird, Birkenhead	19-7-1943

Notes
March 1946 Devonport/Milford Haven Reserve. Aug 1947 Devonport Reserve. Oct 1951-54 converted to Type 15 Frigate by White at Cowes. 23 July 1954 Commissioned for 2nd Training Squadron, Portland. March 1958 Commissioned for 6th FS. 1959 helicopter pad fitted for trials with Wasp helicopter. 1960-61 20th FS, Londonderry. Oct 1961-March 1962 refit at Rosyth, 16 Feb 1962 commissioned for 2nd FS, Portland. 1964-67 long refit at Chatham. 1969 — 5 months refit at Chatham. March 1973 paid off for disposal. Nov 1978 sunk as target by torpedo from "SWIFTSURE" in the Atlantic.

SHIP	BUILDERS	LAUNCH DATE
URSA	J.I. Thornycroft, Southampton	22-7-1943

Notes
1946-52 Portsmouth Reserve. 1952 Chatham Reserve. 1953-55 converted to Type 15 Frigate by Palmers, Tyne. 29 June 1955 Commissioned for 6th FS in Mediterranean. April 1959 to Malta for refit (work suspended after 6 weeks). 1959-61 Malta Reserve. 11 Nov 1961 commissioned for 5th FS. 1 Aug 1962 bows damaged in collision with "BATTLEAXE" during night exercises in Clyde. March 1963 relieved "TROUBRIDGE" in 8th FS. 28 Oct 1966 paid off at Devonport. 23 Sept 1967 towed from Devonport for Newport to be broken up.

HMS Ursa (March 1946)

"V" CLASS

Displacement (tons) 1,710 **Length** 352 ft. 9 ins. **Beam** 35 ft. 8 ins. **Draught** 10 ft. **Speed** 36 knots **Amament** 4 x 4.7"; 4 x 40mm A.A.; 2 to 4 x 20mm A.A. **Torpedo Tubes** 8 x 21" (quadruple mountings) **Complement** 180

SHIP	BUILDERS	LAUNCH DATE
VIGILANT	Swan Hunter, Wallsend	22-12-1942

Notes
Jan 1946 Londonderry Flotilla. Sept 1946 to the Mediterranean. 1947-51 Portsmouth Reserve. 1951-52, converted to Type 15 Frigate by Thornycroft, Woolston. Sept 1953-55 6th FS Home Fleet. 27 Oct 1954 collided with "RELENTLESS" off West Coast of Scotland. Repaired at Devonport. 1955 refitted as Training Frigate. Nov 1956 Dartmouth Training Squadron. July 1963 Devonport Reserve. 4 June 1965 arrived Faslane to be broken up.

SHIP	BUILDERS	LAUNCH DATE
VIRAGO	Swan Hunter, Wallsend	4-2-1943

Notes
1946-49 3rd DF Mediterranean. 1949-51 Chatham Reserve. 1952-53 converted to Type 15 Frigate at Chatham. 1953-54 6th FS Home Fleet. 1955-60 Chatham Reserve. 1962-63 17th FS. 1963-64 Devonport Reserve. 4 June 1965 arrived Faslane to be broken up.

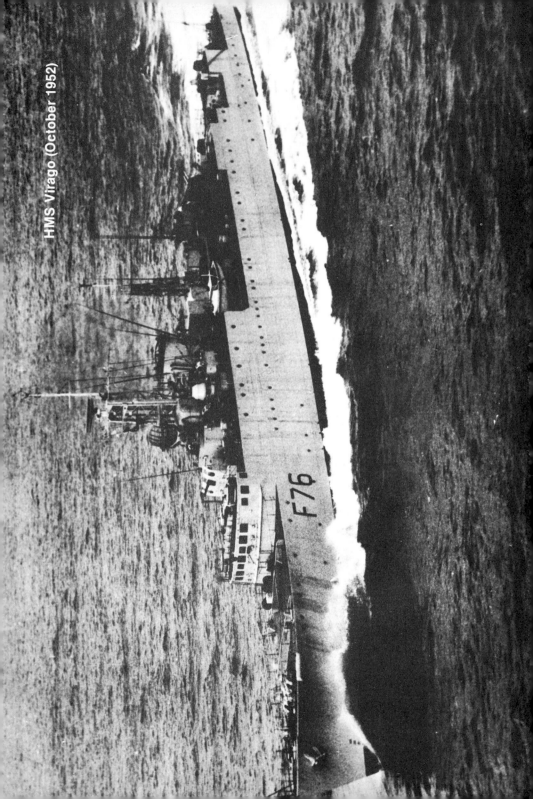

HMS Virago (October 1952)

HMS Verulam (January 1945)

SHIP	BUILDERS	LAUNCH DATE
VENUS	Fairfield, Govan	23-2-1943

Notes
1946-49 3rd DF in Mediterranean. 1949-51 Devonport Reserve. 1951-52 Converted to Type 15 Frigate at Devonport. 1952-54 6th FS Home Fleet. 1955 refitted for Dartmouth Training Squadron. 1964 to Reserve. Oct 1969 Target Ship (ship to ship effect of Seadart missile). 20 Dec 1972 arrived Briton Ferry to be broken up.

SHIP	BUILDERS	LAUNCH DATE
VERULAM	Fairfield, Govan	22-4-1943

Notes
1946 Londonderry Flotilla. Feb 1947-March 1949 3rd DF in Mediterranean. 1951-52 converted to Type 15 Frigate at Portsmouth. Sept 1954 Portsmouth Reserve. 1958-61 A.S.W.E. Trials Ship. 1961 2nd FS Portland Trails Ship for U.W.D.E. 21 Dec 1970 paid off for disposal. 23 Oct 1972 arrived Newport to be broken up.

SHIP	BUILDERS	LAUNCH DATE
VOLAGE	J.S. White, Cowes	15-12-1943

Notes
1946-49 3rd DF in Mediterranean. 22 Oct 1946 went to the aid of "SAUMAREZ" when mined in Corfu Channel. Took her in tow, but she herself struck a mine. Bows blown off. Towed to Malta for repairs. 17 May 1949 arrived Portsmouth from Mediterranean. 1949-52 Portsmouth Reserve. 1952 converted to Type 15 Frigate by Whites, Cowes. Sept 1954 3rd TS, Londonderry. 1956-58 Portsmouth Reserve. 1960 Rosyth Reserve. 1964 Harbour Training Ship at Portsmouth (for Royal Marines). 1966-72 laid up a Portsmouth. 1972 sold to Portsmouth Shipbreakers.

HMS Volage (May 1949)

"W" CLASS

Displacement (tons) 1,710 (KEMPENFELT 1,730 tons) **Length** 362 ft. 9 ins. **Beam** 35ft. 9 ins. **Draught** 10 ft. **Speed** 36 knots **Armament** 4 x 4.7"; 4 x 40mm A.A.; 4 x 20mm A.A. **Torpedo Tubes** 8 x 21" (quadruple mountings) **Complement** 186

SHIP	BUILDERS	LAUNCH DATE
KEMPENFELT (EX-VALENTINE)	John Brown, Clydebank	8-5-1943

Notes
1946-47 Chatham Reserve. 1948-53 Simonstown Reserve. 1953-55 Portsmouth Reserve. 1956 sold to Yugoslavia and renamed "KOTOR". 1970 broken up at Split.

SHIP	BUILDERS	LAUNCH DATE
WHELP	Hawthorn Leslie, Hebburn	3-6-1943

Notes
1946-47 Portsmouth Reserve. 28 Nov 1947 left Portsmouth for Reserve at Simonstown. 1952 transferred to South Africa and renamed "SIMON VAN DER STEL". 1961 in Reserve. 1962 taken in hand for modernisation. 18 Feb 1964 commissioned. 1976 disposal list.

HMS Whelp (November 1947)

SHIP	BUILDERS	LAUNCH DATE
WAKEFUL (EX-ZEBRA)	Fairfield, Govan	30-6-1943

Notes

Jan 1946 at Portsmouth, CW Training Ship. Sept 1948-49 Rosyth — Boy's Training Ship and Local Flotilla. 1950-51 Rosyth 4th Training Flotilla. April 1951-53 conversion to Type 15 Frigate by Scotts, Greenock. 1953-57 5th FS Mediterranean. 16 May 1957 returned to Portsmouth; taken in hand for conversion to Radar and Nav. Training Ship. Nov 1959 replaced "STARLING" in Portsmouth Squadron. April 1964 2nd FS, and Tender to "DRYAD". 1966-67 fitted with experimental satellite terminal and stabilisers for trails. 1969 replace by "GRENVILLE". 26 Feb 1970 left Portsmouth for de-equipping at Rosyth. 5 May 1971 arrived Inverkeithing to be broken up.

SHIP	BUILDERS	LAUNCH DATE
WHIRLWIND	Hawthorn Leslie, Hebburn	30-8-1943

Notes

Jan 1946 at Chatham — CW Training Ship. 1947-48 Rosyth — Boy's Training Ship and Local Flotilla. 1952-53 converted to Type 15 Frigate by Palmers. 28 July 1953 commissioned for 5th FS in Mediterranean and Home Waters. 1956 Cyprus patrols and Suez crisis. June 1959-May 1961 refit at Rosyth. 11 July 1961 commissioned for 8th FS in Home/West Indies. 1966 approved to scrap. 12 Sept 1969 towed from Portsmouth to Pembroke Dock for use as target. 29 Oct 1974 foundered at her moorings in Cardigan Bay, became a total loss.

SHIP	BUILDERS	LAUNCH DATE
WESSEX (EX-ZENITH)	Fairfield, Govan	2-9-1943

Notes

Jan 1946-47 Devonport Reserve. 1948-50 Simonstown Reserve. 29 March 1950 transferred to South Africa. Renamed "JAN VAN RIEBEECK". 1961 in Reserve. 1964 taken in hand at Simonstown for modernisation; completed 1966. 1978 Disposal list.

HMS Wakeful (June 1950)

HMS Whirlwind (February 1947)

SHIP	BUILDERS	LAUNCH DATE
WIZARD	V. Armstrong, Barrow	29-9-1943

Notes

Feb 1946-51 Plymouth Local Flotilla. 1953-54 converted to Type 15 Frigate at Devonport Dockyard. 1954-57 5th FS in Mediterranean. 1960 refitted at Chatham for Dartmouth Training Squadron role. 1962 8th FS, West Indies. 1964-66 Dartmouth Training Squadron. 7 March 1967 arrived Inverkeithing to be broken up.

SHIP	BUILDERS	LAUNCH DATE
WAGER	John Brown, Clydebank	1-11-1943

Notes

Jan 1946-47 Portsmouth Reserve. 1948-55 Simonstown Reserve. 1956 Sold to Yugoslavia and renamed "PULA". 1971 Disposal list.

SHIP	BUILDERS	LAUNCH DATE
WRANGLER	V. Armstrong, Barrow	30-12-1943

Notes

Jan 1946 Devonport CW Training Ship. Sept 1946-50 Rosyth Local Flotilla and Boy's Training Ship. June 1950 4th TF, Rosyth. 1951-53 converted to Type 15 Frigate, by Harland & Wolff at Liverpool. Sept 1953-55 5th FS in Mediterranean. 1956 refitted at Cardiff. 29 Nov 1956 transferred to South Africa. Renamed "VRYSTAAT". April 1976 sunk as a target.

**HMS Wrangler
(March 1955)**

HMS Wizard (April 1944)

"Z" CLASS

Displacement (tons) 1,710 **Length** 362 ft. 9 ins. **Beam** 35 ft. 9 ins. **Draught** 10 ft. **Speed** 36 knots **Armament** 4 x 4.5";2 x 40mm A.A.; 6 x 20mm A.A. **Torpedo Tubes** 8 x 21" (quadruple mountings) **Complement** 186

All were due for conversion to Type 15 Frigates — but only ZEST was eventually converted.

SHIP	BUILDERS	LAUNCH DATE
MYNGS	V. Armstrong, Tyne	31-5-1943

Notes
June 1946-Aug 1947 4th DF, Home Fleet. Aug 1948 3rd EF, Portland. April 1949-Aug 1954 2nd TF, Portland. Sept 1954 placed in Reserve pending conversion. But . . . May 1955 transferred to Egypt and renamed "EL QAHER". 1955 refitted by White, Cowes. 28 Aug 1956 sailed for Egypt. May 1963-July 1964 refitted by White, Cowes. 16 May 1970 sunk by Israeli aircraft at Berenice.

SHIP	BUILDERS	LAUNCH DATE
ZEPHYR	V. Armstrong, Tyne	15-7-1943

Notes
Aug 1946-May 1947 4th DF, Home Fleet. July 1947-Feb 1948 Portsmouth Flotilla as Gunnery Ship. Feb 1948 3rd EF, Porland. Feb 1949 Leader of 2nd TF. 1954-58 Portsmouth Reserve, 2 July 1958 arrived Dunston to be broken up.

HMS Myngs (July 1950)

HMS Zest (April 1952)

SHIP	BUILDERS	LAUNCH DATE
ZEST	J.I. Thornycroft, Southampton	14-10-1943

Notes

Sept-Nov 1945 Refitted at Leith. Aug 1946-Feb 1947 4th DF — Home Fleet. Feb 1947 Reduced to Reserve at Sheerness. July 1947-Feb1948 Portsmouth Flotilla — Torpedo Training. 1948-49 Portland. May 1952 Nore Local Flotilla. Sept 1952-Feb 1954 Chatham Reserve. Feb 1954-March 1956 converted to Type 15 Frigate at Chatham. 1956-58 3rd TS, Londonderry. 1958-61 4th FS. 1961 Malta refit. 1964 24th ES. July 1968 paid off to Reserve at Plymouth. Aug 1970 towed from Devonport to Dalmuir to be broken up.

SHIP	BUILDERS	LAUNCH DATE
ZAMBESI	Cammell Laird, Birkenhead	21-11-1943

Notes

1946 4th DF, Home Fleet. 1946-50 Devonport Reserve. Feb 1948 refit at Gibraltar. 1951-51 Target Ship for 3rd Submarine Flotilla, Rothesay. 1953-54 Refit at Penarth. 1954-59 in Reserve at Cardiff. 12 Feb 1959 arrived Briton Ferry to be broken up.

SHIP	BUILDERS	LAUNCH DATE
ZEALOUS	Cammell Laird, Birkenhead	28-2-1944

Notes

Oct 1945-Aug 1946 2nd DF in Home Fleet. 1947-50 Devonport Reserve. 1950-51 Refit at Cardiff. 1953-54 in Reserve at Penarth. 15 July 1955 transferred to Israel — at Cardiff — renamed "ELATH". 1956 refitted by Harland & Wolff at Liverpool. 21 Oct 1967 sunk by 3 missiles from Egyptian patrol boats off the Sinai Coast.

HMS Zambezi (June 1951)

SHIP	BUILDERS	LAUNCH DATE
ZEBRA	Wm. Denny, Dumbarton	8-3-1944

Notes
1946 4th DF, Home Fleet. 1947-50 Devonport Reserve. 1951-52 Harwich Reserve. 1954 Devonport Reserve. 1954-55 conversion to Type 15 Frigate considered; main armament removed, but placed on Sales List. 1957 examined by West German Navy, but ship reported in "poor" condition. 12 Feb 1959 arrived Newport to be broken up.

SHIP	BUILDERS	LAUNCH DATE
ZODIAC	J.I. Thornycroft, Southampton	11-3-1944

Notes
1946 2nd DF. 1947-48 Portsmouth Reserve. 1949 2nd TF, Portland. 1952 Portsmouth Reserve. March 1954 Refit at Penarth then Reserve at Cardiff. 15 July 1955 at Cardiff handed over to Israel and renamed "YAFFO". Refitted by Crichton, Liverpool. 1956 sailed for Isreal. 1972 withdrawn from service.

SHIP	BUILDERS	LAUNCH DATE
ZENITH (EX-WESSEX)	Wm. Denny, Dumbarton	5-6-1944

Notes
1946 4th DF, Home Fleet. 1947-50 Reserve at Chatham. 17 Oct 1950 towed from Chatham for refit by Palmer, Tyne. 1951-54 Harwich Reserve. May 1955 sold to Egypt and renamed "EL FATEH". Refitted by Thornycroft, Woolston. 30 August 1956 sailed to Egypt. May 1963-July 1964 modernised by White, Cowes. Still in service 1980.

HMS Zenith (August 1943)

HMS Zodiac (January 1952)

'C' Class — "CA" Group

HMS Caprice — The last 'proper' destroyer makes her last port visit — Swansea April 1973.

Displacement (tons) 1,710 **Length** 362 ft. 9 ins. **Beam** 35 ft. 9 ins. **Draught** 10 ft. **Speed** 34 knots **Armament** 4 x 4.5", 4 x 40mm A.A., 4 x 20mm **Torpedo Tubes** 8 x 21" (quadruple mountings) **Complement** 186 (Cavendish 222)

From 1945 to May 1946 all CA's were in the 6th D.F. in the Indian Ocean. They then returned home to operational Reserve. Most spent about 10 years in Reserve and were then modernised.

SHIP	BUILDERS	LAUNCH DATE
CAPRICE (Ex-Swallow)	Yarrow, Scotstoun	16-9-1943

Notes

Modernised by Yarrow. March 1959 — Commissioned for 8th D.S. Served East of Suez for 4 years. 1963 transferred to 21st E.S. Nov 1963-June 1966 refit (fitted with "Seacat") then placed in Reserve at Rosyth. 1966-68 two deployments to Far East. Feb 1969 to Reserve at Gibraltar. 1971-73 Sea-going training ship for Engineer Officers at Devonport. Mar 1973 paid off for disposal at Devonport. 5 Oct 1973 arrived Queensborough to be broken up.

HMS Cassandra (July 1961)

SHIP	BUILDERS	LAUNCH DATE
CASSANDRA (Ex-Tourmaline)	Yarrow, Scotstoun	29-11-1943

Notes
Modernised by Yarrow. Apr 1960 8th D.S. in Far East. Feb 1963 21st D.S. in Mediterranean. 1964-65 in Mediterranean and Far East. Jan 1966 paid off and laid up at Portsmouth. 28 Apr 1967 arrived Inverkeithing to be broken up.

HMS Cambrian (October 1944)

SHIP	BUILDERS	LAUNCH DATE
CAMBRIAN (Ex-Spitfire)	Scotts, Greenock	10-12-1943

Notes

Jan 1963 commissioned at Devonport for service with 22nd E.S. 1963-68 Three commissions in Home/Far Eastern waters. Dec 1968 paid off at Portsmouth. Sept 1971 arrived Briton Ferry to be broken up.

HMS Caesar (1964)

SHIP	BUILDERS	LAUNCH DATE
CAESAR (Ex-Ranger)	John Brown, Clydebank	14-2-1944

Notes

1957-60 long refit at Rosyth. Sept 1960 commissioned as leader of 8th D.S. 1960-65 in Far East as leader of 8th D.S., 24th E.S. and 26th E.S. June 1965 paid off and de-equipped at Chatham. 6 Jan 1967 arrived Blyth to be broken up.

SHIP	BUILDERS	LAUNCH DATE
CARRON (EX-STRENUOUS)	Scotts, Greenock	28-3-1944

Notes

Aug 1955 completed conversion at Chatham. A deckhouse had replaced "B" gun. Joined Dartmouth Training Squadron. Oct 1957 rest of armament removed. Sept 1958 re-joined Dartmouth T.S. July 1960 transferred to Portsmouth and employed as Navigation Training Ship. March 1963 paid off for disposal. 4 April 1967 arrived Inverkeithing to be broken up.

90

HMS Cavalier (June 1946)

SHIP	BUILDERS	LAUNCH DATE
CAVALIER (EX-PELLEW)	J.S. White, Cowes	7-4-1944

Notes

Modernised by Thornycroft. Sept 1957 commissioned for 8th DS in Far East, served there 6 years. July 1963 to Reserve at Chatham. 21 May 1964 under tow to Gibraltar, was badly damaged in collision with Liberian tanker "BURGAN". Towed back to Portsmouth for temporary repairs, then to Devonport for fitting of complete new bow. Aug 1964-Jan 1966 refit at Gibraltar; (fitted with "Seacat"). 1967-68 Far East. 1970-72 4th FS in Home Waters. July 1972 paid off at Chatham pending preservation plans. 1974 proposed she be retained as a museum ship. 1977 sold to H.M.S. Cavalier Trust for £65,000. Towed from Chatham 11 Oct 1977. After a few days at Portsmouth, was towed to Southampton 21 Oct 1977. Where she became a museum ship. (June 1982)

SHIP	BUILDERS	LAUNCH DATE
CAVENDISH (Ex-Sibyl)	John Brown, Clydebank	12-4-1944

Notes

Spring 1956 modernisation completed and joined 6th D.S. 1956-59 Two Home/Med commissions. 1959-61 Far East. July 1961-Aug 1962 refit at Gibraltar then joined 25th E.S. Nov 1963 joined 21st E.S. for 9 months East of Suez. 1964 laid up at Portsmouth. March 1965 taken in hand for long refit. 3 June 1966 towed from Portsmouth to Chatham. 17 Aug 1967 arrived Blyth for breaking up.

SHIP	BUILDERS	LAUNCH DATE
CARYSFORT (Ex-Pique)	J.S. White, Cowes	25-7-1944

Notes

Spring 1956 modernisation completed and joined 6th D.S. 1956-59 Two Home/Med commissions. Nov 1962-May 1964 refit at Gibraltar then joined 27th E.S. and spent 2 deployments in Med. Oct 1967-Oct 1968 Far East. Feb 1969 paid off. Nov 1970 arrived Newport to be broken up.

HMS Cavendish (September 1957)

HMS Carysfort (March 1957)

'C' Class — "CH" Group

Displacement (tons) 1,710 Length 362 ft. 9 ins. Beam 35 ft. 9 ins. Draught 10 ft. Speed 34 knots Armament 4 x 4.5", 4 x 40mm A.A., 4 x 20mm Torpedo Tubes 8 x 21" (quadruple mountings) Complement 186

The 8 ships of this Group formed 14th (afterwards 1st) D.F. in the Mediterranean until 1950.

SHIP	BUILDERS	LAUNCH DATE
CHEVRON	Alex Stephen, Govan	23-2-1944

Notes
1957-64 Operational Reserve at Rosyth, where she was hulked along with "Duncansby Head" and "Girdle Ness" to form "Cochrane" Accommodation Group. Dec 1969 arrived Inverkeithing to be broken up.

SHIP	BUILDERS	LAUNCH DATE
CHEVIOT	Alex Stephen, Govan	2-5-1944

Notes
Dec 1956 - Oct 1959 in Far East with 8th D.S. March 1960 replaced the frigate "Talybont" as Harbour Training Ship at Rosyth (attached to "Caledonia"). 22nd Oct 1962 arrived at Inverkeithing to be broken up.

SHIP	BUILDERS	LAUNCH DATE
CHAPLET	J.I. Thornycroft, Southampton	18-7-1944

Notes
1951 to Reserve. 1953 rejoined 1st D.S. Feb 1959 recommissioned into Devonport Local Squadron. Sept 1961 paid off at Devonport. 6 Nov 1965 sold to Hughes Bolckow, Blyth.

HMS Chevron (November 1959)

HMS Cheviot (January 1950)

HMS Chaplet (July 1950)

HMS Chequers (September 1945)

SHIP	BUILDERS	LAUNCH DATE
CHEQUERS	Scotts, Greenock	30-10-1944

Notes
Nov 1954 Operational Reserve at Portsmouth. Feb 1964 Disposal list at Portsmouth. 23 July 1966 arrived Newport to be broken up.

SHIP	BUILDERS	LAUNCH DATE
CHARITY	J.I. Thornycroft, Southampton	30-11-1944

Notes
1951-54 8th D.S. in Far East. 1955 paid off. 16 Dec 1958 sold to Pakistan Navy; renamed "Shah Jehan". (Still in service 1980).

SHIP	BUILDERS	LAUNCH DATE
CHIEFTAIN	Scotts, Greenock	26-2-1945

Notes
1953 to reserve. 20 Mar 1961 arrived Sunderland to be broken up.

SHIP	BUILDERS	LAUNCH DATE
CHILDERS	Wm. Denny, Dumbarton	27-2-1945

Notes
1951 to Reserve. 1958 laid up at Gibraltar. 14 Sept 1963 left Gibraltar in tow of Dutch tug "Noordzee". 22 Sept 1963 arrived Spezia to be broken up.

SHIP	BUILDERS	LAUNCH DATE
CHIVALROUS	Wm. Denny, Dumbarton	22-6-1945

Notes
29 June 1954 sold to Pakistan Navy and renamed "Taimur". 1961 broken up.

HMS Chieftain (March 1946)

'C' Class — "CO" Group

HMS Cockade

Details as for "CH" Group

1946-47 Eight ships of "CO" Group formed 8th D.S. in Far East. 1948 COMET and CONTEST reduced to Reserve. The other six served in the Korean War.

SHIP	BUILDERS	LAUNCH DATE
COCKADE	Yarrow, Scotstoun	7-3-1944

Notes
1947-57 in Far East. 1958 paid off. Sept 1964 arrived Newport to be broken up.

SHIP	BUILDERS	LAUNCH DATE
COSSACK	V. Armstrong, Tyne	10-5-1944

Notes
Dec 1959 arrived Devonport after 14 years in Far East. 1 March 1961 arrived Troon to be broken up.

HMS Comet (Note mines on stern)

HMS Consort

SHIP	BUILDERS	LAUNCH DATE
COMET	Yarrow, Scotstoun	22-6-1944

Notes
1953-57 6th D.S. in Home Fleet. Feb 1958 paid off. 23 Oct 1962 arrived Troon to be broken up.

SHIP	BUILDERS	LAUNCH DATE
CONSTANCE	V. Armstrong, Tyne	22-8-1944

Notes
8 March 1956 arrived Inverkeithing to be broken up.

SHIP	BUILDERS	LAUNCH DATE
CONSORT	Alex Stephen, Govan	19-10-1944

Notes
1947-57 Foreign Service, mainly in Far East. 15 March 1961 arrived Swansea to be broken up.

HMS Contest (November 1945)

SHIP	BUILDERS	LAUNCH DATE
CONTEST	J.S. White, Cowes	16-12-1944

Notes
1951 Torpedo Training Ship at Portsmouth. 1955 — 6th D.S. 2nd Feb 1960 arrived Grays, Essex to be broken up.

SHIP	BUILDERS	LAUNCH DATE
COMUS	J.I. Thornycroft, Southampton	14-3-1945

Notes
Proposed sale to Peru cancelled. 12 Nov 1958 arrived Newport to be broken up.

SHIP	BUILDERS	LAUNCH DATE
CONCORD (Ex-Corso)	J.I. Thornycroft, Southampton	14-5-1945

Notes
Renamed Concord in June 1946. 1947-57 in Far East. 1957 withdrawn from active service. Attached to 'Caledonia' at Rosyth as Harbour Training Ship. 22 Oct 1962 arrived Inverkeithing to be broken up.

HMS Comus (November 1951)

'C' Class — "CR" Group

HMS Crispin (June 1953)

Details as for "CH" Group

Only two of the "CR" Group served in the R.N. — CREOLE and CRISPIN. CRESCENT and CRUSADER were transferred to R.C.N. on completion in 1945. Others were transferred to Norway when completed in 1946.

SHIP	BUILDERS	LAUNCH DATE
CROZIERS	Yarrow, Scotstoun	19-9-1944

Notes
Sold to Norway 10 Oct 1946; renamed "Trondheim". Removed from Active List May 1961.

SHIP	BUILDERS	LAUNCH DATE
CRYSTAL	Yarrow, Scotstoun	12-2-1945

Notes
Sold to Norway 10 Oct 1946; renamed "Stavanger". 1967 Disposal List.

SHIP	BUILDERS	LAUNCH DATE
CRISPIN (Ex-Craccher)	J.S. White, Cowes	23-6-1945

Notes
Renamed "Crispen" in June 1946. 1946 4th E.F., later 3rd T.S. at Londonderry. 1954 paid off. 18 Mar 1958 sold to Pakistan; renamed "Jahangir", after refit by J.I. Thornycroft, Southampton. (Still in service 1980.)

SHIP	BUILDERS	LAUNCH DATE
CRETAN	Scotts, Greenock	6-8-1945

Notes
Renamed "Cromwell" in June, 1946. July 1946 sold to Norway; renamed "Bergen". 1967 Disposal List.

SHIP	BUILDERS	LAUNCH DATE
CREOLE	J.S. White, Cowes	22-11-1945

Notes
1946 4th E.F., later 3rd T.S. at Londonderry. 1953 paid off. 1956 sold to Pakistan. 20 June 1958 transferred at Southampton and renamed "Alamgir". (Still in service 1980.)

SHIP	BUILDERS	LAUNCH DATE
CROWN	Scotts, Greenock	19-12-1945

Notes
July 1946 sold to Norway; renamed "Oslo". Jan 1964 transferred to Reserve. 1966 Disposal List.

'C' Class — "CE" Group

A fifth Group of this Class was planned but only two materialised. CELT and CENTAUR were redesigned and laid down as the Weapon Class SWORD and TOMAHAWK. TOMAHAWK was renamed SCORPION in Jan 1946. SWORD was cancelled on 5 Oct 1945.

EARLY (or 1942) BATTLE CLASS

HMS Sluys (September 1946)

The 1942 Battles represented the first break from the standard wartime design of fleet destroyer-typified by the O-CR classes. The requirements of the Pacific war, and the need for better A/A capability, meant that the Battles were considerably larger than earlier destroyers and were fitted with the new twin 4.5″ mountings and a large number of Bofors guns. Intended for war service against Japan, but only six out of sixteen ships were sent to the Pacific. However, these ships, together with the eight "1943 ships" made up a considerable part of the Royal Navy's destroyer force until the 1960's.

The first, BARFLEUR, completed in September 1944, joined the British Pacific Fleet in time to see service against Japan. After VJ Day she was joined by ARMADA, CAMPERDOWN, HOGUE, LAGOS and TRAFALGAR to form the 19th Destroyer Flotilla. Two other ships intended for this flotilla, SOLEBAY and FINISTERRE, were retained in home waters. Early in 1947 the 19DF was withdrawn from the Far East and all six ships were placed in reserve. Ten years passed before TRAFALGAR, CAMPERDOWN, HOGUE and LAGOS recommissioned.

The second flotilla — of ships completed in 1946 — was kept in the Home Fleet as the 5th DF. Led by SOLEBAY, HM Ships CADIZ, GABBARD, ST JAMES, ST KITTS and SLUYS served in the Home Fleet until 1953. SAINTES then replaced SOLEBAY as gunnery training ship at Portsmouth with FINISTERRE. The remaining two ships, GRAVELINES and VIGO, were placed in reserve after completion. A further "Battle Flotilla" was formed in July 1949 when SAINTES, ARMADA, VIGO and GRAVELINES replaced the V class as the 3rd DF in the Mediterranean.

No further changes took place until 1953. The advent of the "Darings" spelt the demise of the 5DS and all six ships went into reserve after the Coronation Review. Only two, ST KITTS and SOLEBAY, saw further service in the Royal Navy. Earlier in 1953 BARFLEUR had replaced GRAVELINES and ARMADA in the 3rd DS. In 1954 VIGO left 3DS being replaced by ST KITTS. VIGO was required to replace FINISTERRE at Portsmouth as gunnery training ship — a role she carried out until August 1959. After 3DS converted to General Service commissions, ARMADA replaced SAINTES in 1956 when she went to Rosyth for a major refit. At the end of 1956, only four early Battles were in service — VIGO, ARMADA, BARFLEUR and ST KITTS. By 1957/8 however the Battles were back in business . . .

The CH class destroyers of 1st DS were replaced in May 1957 by the newly refited and recommissioned SOLEBAY, HOGUE and LAGOS. The 1DS spent the next 18 months in the Home/Med Fleet. Recommissioned in November 1958 the squadron deployed to the Far East in Apr 1959 — the first Battles on that Station since 1947. The squadron's stay in the Far East was marred by HOGUE's fatal collision with the Indian cruiser MYSORE on 25 August 1959. She was laid up, "damaged beyond repair", at Singapore until scrapped there in 1962. When her two sisters arrived home in April 1960 FINISTERRE joined as HOGUE's replacement. In the following month the 1DS was reconstituted by an amalgamation with the 3DS — as a result LAGOS paid off. Led by SOLEBAY, FINISTERRE, SAINTES and CAMPERDOWN completed a final two year commission as 1DS at Home and in the Med before reduction to reserve in April 1962.

The ships of the 3DS came home in December 1954 and returned to the Med in October 1955 and took part in the Suez operation. They joined the Home Fleet at the end of 1956. On 2 October 1957 ST KITTS was replaced by the newly refitted CAMPERDOWN. A year later BARFLEUR finally paid off and was replaced by SAINTES who also became leader. In the spring of 1960 ARMADA paid off and the other two ships joined the 1DS.

One other early Battle re-entered service in 1958. TRAFALGAR became leader of the newly formed 7DS in May of that year. She spent the next six years rotating between the Home and Med Fleets — serving on the latter station as the last 1942 Battle in service. She paid off in May 1963.

By now the Battles had had their day but some escaped the scrapman for a new lease of life. In 1957 CADIZ and GABBARD were sold to Pakistan and renamed KHAIBAR and BADR respectively. (The former was lost in the war with India December 1971) Early in 1958, GRAVELINES and ST JAMES began refits at Devonport but were abandoned in November 1958. Their hulks were sent to the breakers in 1961. SLUYS ended her 13 years in reserve at Devonport when she was sold to Iran in 1966. Modernised and renamed ARTEMIZ she recommissioned in 1970 as a training ship. After years in reserve at Portsmouth and Devonport respectively, TRAFALGAR and CAMPERDOWN were scrapped in the summer of 1970. Only SAINTES remained. In April 1962 she had been hulked at Rosyth as tender to the CALEDONIA artificers training school. She remained there for ten years, providing a spectacle every Navy Day as she was "blown up" by Marines amidst much steam, smoke and gunfire. She was eventually replaced by DUNCAN in 1972 — and she too headed for the scrapyard.

EARLY BATTLE CLASS

HMS Barfleur (June 1949)

Displacement (tons) 2,315 **Length** 379 ft. **Beam** 40 ft. 3 ins.
Draught 12 ft. 9 ins. **Speed** 34 knots **Armament** 4 x 4.5″, 10 to 14
x 40mm A.A. (ships starred also had 1 x 4″ abaft the funnel)
Torpedo Tubes 8 x 21″ **Complement** 247-308

SHIP	BUILDERS	LAUNCH DATE
BARFLEUR	Swan Hunter	1-11-1943

Notes
29 Sept 1966 arrived Dalmuir to be broken up.

SHIP	BUILDERS	LAUNCH DATE
ARMADA	Hawthorn Leslie	9-12-1943

Notes
18 Dec 1965 arrived Inverkeithing to be broken up.

SHIP	BUILDERS	LAUNCH DATE
TRAFALGAR*	Swan Hunter	12-1-1944

Notes
July 1970 arrived Dalmuir to be broken up.

108

HMS Trafalgar

HMS Camperdown (February 1958)

SHIP	BUILDERS	LAUNCH DATE
CAMPERDOWN	Fairfield	8-2-1944

Notes Sept 1970 arrived Faslane to be broken up.

SHIP	BUILDERS	LAUNCH DATE
SOLEBAY	Hawthorn Leslie	22-2-1944

Notes
July 1953-May 1957 in Reserve at Chatham. 1962 Harbour Training Ship at Portsmouth. 11 Aug 1967 arrived Troon to be broken up.

SHIP	BUILDERS	LAUNCH DATE
HOGUE*	Cammell Laird	21-4-1944

Notes 1 Mar 1962 sold at Singapore to be broken up locally.

SHIP	BUILDERS	LAUNCH DATE
FINISTERRE*	Fairfield	22-6-1944

Notes 12 June 1967 arrived Dalmuir to be broken up.

SHIP	BUILDERS	LAUNCH DATE
SAINTES*	Hawthorn Leslie	19-7-1944

Notes 1 Sept 1972 arrived Cairn Ryan to be broken up.

SHIP	BUILDERS	LAUNCH DATE
LAGOS*	Cammell Laird	4-8-1944

Notes 1 June 1967 towed from Portsmouth to Bo'ness to be broken up.

SHIP	BUILDERS	LAUNCH DATE
CADIZ	Fairfield	16-9-1944

Notes
1 Feb 1957 transferred (at Glasgow) to Pakistan Navy; renamed "Khaibar". Dec 1971 sunk during the Indo-Pakistan war.

HMS Hogue (October 1945)

HMS Finisterre (June 1952)

SHIP	BUILDERS	LAUNCH DATE
ST. KITTS*	Swan Hunter	4-10-1944

Notes
19 Feb 1962 arrived Sunderland to be broken up.

SHIP	BUILDERS	LAUNCH DATE
GRAVELINES*	Cammell Laird	30-11-1944.

Notes
22 Mar 1961 arrived Rosyth to be broken up.

SHIP	BUILDERS	LAUNCH DATE
SLUYS	Cammell Laird	28-2-1945

Notes
2 Jan 1967 arrived Southampton for refit prior to being taken over by Iran. 26 Jan 1967 formally handed over and renamed "Artemiz". (Still in service 1980.)

SHIP	BUILDERS	LAUNCH DATE
GABBARD*	Swan Hunter	16-3-1945

Notes
3 Jan 1956 transferred (at Jarrow) to Pakistan Navy and renamed "Badr". (Still in service 1980.)

SHIP	BUILDERS	LAUNCH DATE
ST JAMES*	Fairfield	7-6-1945

Notes
19 Mar 1961 arrived Newport to be broken up.

SHIP	BUILDERS	LAUNCH DATE
VIGO*	Fairfield	27-9-1945

Notes
6 Dec 1964 arrived Faslane to be broken up.

HMS Cadiz (August 1946)

HMS St. Kitts (September 1948)

HMS Gabbard (May 1946)

HMS Vigo (August 1959)

LATER (OR 1943) BATTLE CLASS

In 1943 twenty-four further Battle class destroyers were ordered — even more ships were planned but were superceded by the "Darings". The principal improvements in the Later Battles were the installation of the American designed Mark 37 director tower and the addition of a single 4.5″ gun abaft the funnel in lieu of two Bofors guns. The conclusion of hostilities, together with delays incurred in the supply of equipment, caused the cancellation of all but eight ships. Seven were broken up on the slip (MONS, OMDURMAN, SOMME, RIVER PLATE, ST. LUCIA, SAN DOMINGO and WATERLOO); five were launched and immediately scrapped (BELLE ISLE, NAVARINO, POICTIERS, TALAVERA and TRINCOMALEE) and four were retained as incomplete hulls for several years after the war (ALBUERA, JUTLAND, NAMUR and OUDENARDE). The hulks of JUTLAND and OUDENARDE lay at Rosyth until scrapped at the end of 1957. Of the eight ships completed, MALPLAQUET was renamed JUTLAND before launching in 1946.

Between November 1946 and May 1948 DUNKIRK, BARROSA, AISNE, JUTLAND, CORUNNA, AGINCOURT, MATAPAN and ALAMEIN were completed for service as the 4th Destroyer Flotilla in the Home Fleet. The 4DF was not to attain its full strength. The manning crisis of October 1947 left the Home Fleet with just four destroyers in service, AGINCOURT, AISNE, DUNKIRK and JUTLAND. The principal casualty of this crisis was MATAPAN — she had just completed builder's trials in the Clyde and had arrived at Devonport for commissioning. Her "temporary" reduction to reserve lasted for 22 years!! She was eventually towed to Portsmouth for conversion to a Sonar Trials Ship in 1970.

By the end of 1948 the flotilla was back in full commission. But a year later another reduction took place. The need for A/S escorts, together with the unsuitability of the Battles for this role brought the decision, in March 1950, to pay off several destroyers in the Home and Mediterranean Fleets and replace them with Loch class frigates. DUNKIRK, BARROSA and ALAMEIN paid off into reserve and AISNE and JUTLAND were "temporarily laid-up" — for almost a year. In 1951 the squadron was back in business. Converted to General Service Commissions, the squadron served in the Mediterranean (December 1954-October 1955). Refitting at the time of Suez, ALAMEIN replaced AISNE in 1957 and a further years GSC deployment to the Med. took place from November 1957. The last month of the squadron's existance was marred by a collision between BARROSA (who had replaced JUTLAND in 1953) and CORUNNA in the Bay of Biscay on 15th March 1959. The 4th DS was then disbanded. ALAMEIN went into reserve and AGINCOURT, BARROSA and CORUNNA into dockyard hands for conversion to radar pickets.

In May 1958 two later Battles recommissioned for service in the newly formed 7th DS. Led by TRAFALGAR, DUNKIRK and JUTLAND served in the Home and Med. Fleets. Two such deployments were completed by the time JUTLAND went back into reserve in the spring of 1961. DUNKIRK completed a further two year commission, being in the Med. April 1962-April 1963. She paid off in May 1963, the last unconverted 1943 Battle in service.

Between 1959 and 1962 four ships were converted to radar pickets. Only the hull, engines, forward superstructure and 4.5″ guns remained of the original ships. A massive lattice mast with "double bedstead" aerial, and remodelled after superstructure and a "Seacat" missile launcher were added. The conversions of

CORUNNA at Rosyth and AISNE at Chatham were completed in February 1962. Both ships joined 7DS in the Med. Early in 1963 they transferred to new Escort Squadrons. CORUNNA completed one commission (in 21ES) which included a deployment to the Far East (Sept 1964-Aug 1965). Refitted at Rosyth from September 1965 she went into operational reserve at Portsmouth in April 1967. There she remained until placed on the Disposal list in 1972.

AISNE had a longer operational career. After a short period with 23ES, she joined 30ES in January 1964 for service in the Med. from April to September 1964, and then onto the Far East (Sept to Dec 1964 and July to Dec 1965). Recommissioned in Jan 1966 she went East of Suez again in Aug 1966. After her return in April 1967 she was sent to the West Indies (Dec 1967 to March 1968). She paid off in August 1968.

AGINCOURT recommissioned at Portsmouth in May 1962. For the next 4½ years she served in Home and Mediterranean waters as a member of 5DS, 23ES and 27ES. She was in Mediterranean waters again from Jan to Sept 1965 and July to Oct 1966. In addition she served in NATO's Standing Naval Force Atlantic from January to May 1966. Reduced to reserve at Portsmouth in October 1966, she was placed on the disposal list in 1972.

In contrast to her sister ships BARROSA proceeded to the Far East on completion of her conversion at Devonport in April 1962. She joined the 8th Destroyer Squadron — later the 24th Escort Squadron. Apart from two spells at home (July 1966 to Aug 1967 and July to Dec 1968) BARROSA spent her whole radar picket career with the Far East Fleet. She paid off in December 1968. After some time at Devonport, she joined her sisters at Portsmouth in 1971 and was "for disposal" in 1972.

The need to replace VERULAM as Sonar Trials Ship at Portland brought about the major conversion and eventual commissioning of MATAPAN. Only the hull and engines remained of the former destroyer. She eventually found a role in the Navy of the seventies — after so many years "waiting in the wings".

HMS Barrosa

HMS Matapan (September 1947)

LATER BATTLE CLASS

Displacement tons 2,480 **Length** 379 ft **Beam** 40 ft. 6 ins.
Draught 12 ft. 9 ins. **Speed** 30½ knots (35¾ as designed)
Armament 5 x 4.5″; 8 x 40mm A.A. **Torpedo Tubes** 10 x 21″
(quintuple mountings) **Complement** 232-268

SHIP	BUILDERS	LAUNCH DATE
BARROSA	John Brown, Clydebank	17-1-1945

Notes
1974 in use at Portsmouth as a stores hulk. 1 Dec 1978 arrived Blyth to be broken up.

SHIP	BUILDERS	LAUNCH DATE
AGINCOURT	Hawthorn Leslie, Hebburn	29-1-1945

Notes
27 Oct 1974 arrived Sunderland to be broken up.

SHIP	BUILDERS	LAUNCH DATE
MATAPAN	John Brown, Clydebank	30-4-1945

Notes
Jan 1971 at Portsmouth Dockyard for conversion to a sonar trials ship. 2 Feb 1973 commissioned and attached to Admiralty Underwater Weapons Establishment at Portland. 1978 Laid up at Portsmouth. 11 Aug 1979 arrived Blyth to be broken up.

SHIP	BUILDERS	LAUNCH DATE
AISNE	V Armstrong, Tyne	12-5-1945

Notes
27 June 1970 arrived Inverkeithing to be broken up.

HMS Matapan (March 1973)

HMS Corruna (June 1953)

A full house at Portland . . .

HMS Agincourt (September 1948)

HMS Jutland (September 1948)

SHIP	BUILDERS	LAUNCH DATE
ALAMEIN	Hawthorn Leslie, Hebburn	28-5-1945

Notes
1 Dec 1964 arrived Blyth to be broken up.

SHIP	BUILDERS	LAUNCH DATE
CORUNNA	Swan Hunter	29-5-1945

Notes
20 Nov 1974 towed from Portsmouth to Sunderland to be broken up. But . . . 11 Sept 1975 arrived Blyth from Sunderland to be broken up.

SHIP	BUILDERS	LAUNCH DATE
DUNKIRK	Alex Stephen, Govan	27-8-1945

Notes
22 Nov 1965 arrived Faslane to be broken up.

SHIP	BUILDERS	LAUNCH DATE
JUTLAND	Alex Stephen, Govan	20-2-1946

Notes
14 May 1965 arrived at Blyth to be broken up.

"Jutland" — the original one launched by Hawthorn Leslie on 2 November, 1945 was renamed J4922 (her contract number) in December, 1945 — and "Oudenarde" were cancelled after launching. Their hulls were used for experimental purposes at Rosyth. They were eventually broken up in October 1957 and December 1957 respectively.

HMS Alamein (May 1948)

WEAPON CLASS HMS Battleaxe (July 1951)

The nineteen ships of the Weapon Class were ordered in the 1943 War Programme in order to make full use of building capacity in shipyards too small to build the Battle Class. The end of the war, together with design modifications to make them fast anti-submarine ships, resulted in the cancellation of all but four. Three ships were launched and sent straight to the breakers (CARRONADE, CULVERIN, CUTLASS), six were scrapped on the stocks (DAGGER, HOWITZER, LONGBOW, RIFLE, SPEAR, SWORD) and the other six were never laid down (CLAYMORE, DIRK, GRENADE, HALBERD, MUSKET, PONIARD). Only BATTLEAXE, CROSSBOW, BROADSWORD and SCORPION were completed.

The four ships entered service between October 1947 and October 1948. After the turmoil of the manning crisis the Weapons made up the 6th Destroyer Flotilla in the Home Fleet. With BATTLEAXE as leader they were the Navy's only fast A/S escorts until the advent of the Type 15/16 destroyer conversions in 1951. The squadron of identical ships was first disrupted in 1953 when BROADSWORD went into reserve (replaced by COMET). A similar change took place two years later when CROSSBOW was succeeded by CONTEST. The squadron then converted from Home Fleet service to the new General Service. BATTLEAXE and SCORPION completed one such commission in the Home and Mediterranean Fleets (deployed to the latter station April 1955-March 1956). In the summer of 1956 the remaining two Weapons went into Reserve being relieved by CAVENDISH and CARYSFORT.

In 1957 the Admiralty needed to provide the fleet with a radar picket capability to supplement the new SALISBURY class frigates. The four Weapons were selected for conversion and taken in hand (BATTLEAXE and BROADSWORD at

HMS Crossbow (March 1948)

HMS Broadsword (May 1962)

HMS Scorpion (October 1947)

G64

Rosyth, CROSSBOW at Chatham and SCORPION at Devonport). The conversion entailed the removal of both sets of torpedo tubes, re-arrangement of armament in the case of the two at Rosyth, the construction of new deckhouses amidships, and most noticeable — the erection of a second lattice mast with a "bedstead" radar aerial in the former forward torpedo position.

BROADSWORD recommissioned in October 1958 and joined the 7th Destroyer Squadron serving the Home and Mediterranean Fleets until February 1963. She deployed to the Med. three times with the 7th DS (December 1958-April 1959, March 1960-March 1961, April 1962-January 1963) and then paid off into reserve.

BATTLEAXE emerged from Rosyth in February 1959 to join up with Darings of the 2nd DS in the Mediterranean. She returned home in April 1960 and transferred to the other Daring group (the 5th DS) in January 1961. Her service with this squadron was abruptly terminated in August 1962. During a night exercise in the Firth of Clyde she was damaged during a collision with URSA. Although the damage was not excessive, she was paid off as "damaged beyond repair".

CROSSBOW rejoined the fleet in April 1959 and was paired with BATTLEAXE throughout her career as a radar picket but by January 1963 she was reduced to operational reserve. SCORPION, the last to recommission, was similarly paired with BROADSWORD for 3½ years in the 7th DS until she too went into reserve in April 1963. The conversion of the Later Battle class to radar pickets made the Weapons surplus to requirements — hence their comparatively short service (1958-1963) after major refits.

Although their active careers were over, the Weapons Class still performed useful functions. After a year at Rosyth in the hands of the Naval Constructional Research Establishment (NCRE) which tests the ability of ships to withstand damage, BATTLEAXE was scrapped in 1964. After five years in low category reserve at Portsmouth, BROADSWORD went out with a bang when she was blown up in underwater explosive tests, together with ROEBUCK — again for the NCRE at Rosyth. A similar fate befell SCORPION which arrived at Rosyth from Devonport. Two years later she was towed across to Bo'ness for scrap. After three years in operational reserve at Portsmouth, CROSSBOW replaced SOLEBAY as harbour training ship for SULTAN — a duty performed until she was replaced by DIAMOND early in 1970. Two years later she too was scrapped.

WEAPON CLASS

Displacement (tons) 2,280 **Length** 365 ft. **Beam** 38 ft. **Draught** 13 ft. 3 ins. **Speed** 34 knots (as designed) **Armament** 4 x 4" (in twin mountings); 6 x 40mm A.A. **Torpedo Tubes** 10 x 21" (quintuple mountings) — Removed 1958-59. **Complement** 234 (BATTLEAXE 256)

SHIP	BUILDERS	LAUNCH DATE
BATTLEAXE	Yarrow, Scotstoun	12-6-1945

Notes
1 Aug 1962 badly damaged in collision at sea with frigate "URSA". Found, on survey, to be beyond economical repair. Approved for scrapping in 1963 and moored alongside N.C.R.E Rosyth. 20 Oct 1964 arrived Blyth to be broken up.

SHIP	BUILDERS	LAUNCH DATE
CROSSBOW	J. Thornycroft, Southampton	20-12-1945

Notes
11 Dec 1963 left Chatham in tow for Portsmouth to be placed in reserve. 1966 replaced "SOLEBAY" as training ship attached to "SULTAN". 21 Jan 1972 arrived Briton Ferry to be broken up.

SHIP	BUILDERS	LAUNCH DATE
BROADSWORD	Yarrow, Scotstoun	5-2-1946

Notes
25 April 1968 towed from Portsmouth for Rosyth to be used for target trials. 8 Oct 1968 arrived Inverkeithing to be broken up.

SHIP	BUILDERS	LAUNCH DATE
SCORPION	J.S. White, Cowes	15-8-1946

Notes
1955 a new Type 'A' turret was fitted experimentally. Later removed. 27 Sept 1967 left Devonport under tow for Rosyth. 1971 broken up at Bo'ness.

DARING CLASS   HMS Decoy (June 1953)

Sixteen ships of the Daring class were ordered under the 1944 construction programme. Incorporating the heavy gun and torpedo armament of the Battle class and machinery layout of the Weapon class, the Darings represented the ultimate orthodox destroyer design.

Eight ships were cancelled at the end of the war and some names were rearranged to perpetuate the names of the D class destroyers of the early 1930's. Construction was so slow that the eight ships did not enter service until 1952-54, by which time completely new ideas on naval warfare were developing. Loudly praised when first completed as "a most ingenious and comprehensive light warship class" with "The finest anti-aircraft and anti-submarine systems", "Habitability and layout of accommodation are the best possible". — The Admiralty refused to classify them as mere destroyers — they were "Daring class ships" — a hybrid between cruiser and destroyer. In practise the life of the class was rather short — all were withdrawn from service by the end of 1969.

Designed for an earlier age, they proved unadaptable and unpopular. The heavy gun and torpedo armament and very weak ASW capability (1-Squid mortar) were unsuited to the 1960's. With large crews in an age of scarce volunteer sailors, they were cramped and uncomfortable ships. In hull dimensions little larger than the later frigates — they had to accommodate a crew twice as large. The class had a distinct division between ships. Four ships (DECOY, DIAMOND, DIANA,

128

HMS Daring (March 1952)

DUCHESS) had new AC electrical equipment while the other four had an older DC system. The AC group had longer and more active careers, while all four DC ships were scrapped early.

The DC group was allocated to the Med. Fleet — they would have formed the 2nd DS, but thanks to their upgrading to "Darings" they were deployed as an un-numbered group. In 1954, like the other destroyer and frigate squadrons, they converted to the new "general service" commissions. Until January 1958 the DC group alternated with the AC group between the Home and Med. Fleets. DAINTY spent a year in reserve 1955-56 but rejoined her sisters early in 1956. In 1953-54 DEFENDER was detached from her group to the Far East, returning a few months later — the first Daring to go East of Suez. In 1956 the Suez crisis found the group at home, but DARING and DEFENDER were sent out to join the AC group in that ill-fated enterprise.

This group was then refitted between January 1958 and January 1959 (DARING and DELIGHT at Devonport, DAINTY at Portsmouth and DEFENDER at Chatham). The requirement for extra accommodation entailed the removal of the after set of torpedo tubes and the construction of a deckhouse in lieu. Thereafter the DC group, now officially known as the 2nd Destroyer Squadron, did a two year commission in Home/Mediterranean waters. They deployed to the Med. from April 1959-April 1960. In January 1961 the whole group paid off into reserve.

The remaining service of the DC group was limited. All spent some time in reserve and only commissioned for brief periods. DAINTY, refitted from 1962-64 and recommissioned at Portsmouth in April 1965. In a varied two year commission with the 23rd Escort Squadron she not only went to the Mediterranean but also spent four months in the West Indies in the winter of 1965-66. Recommissioned in April 1967, her final period of service was spent in Home, West Indian and Far Eastern waters. On her return from the latter in June 1969, after only nine months East of Suez, she paid off for disposal when only 16 years old. (Having served on board for this commission it was the only answer. She was in a bad way!)

DEFENDER also recommissioned in 1965. After four years in reserve at Chatham, including a year's refit, she too joined the 23rd Escort Squadron in March 1965. There followed one Home/Med. commission, including a few months in the West Indies (1966-67) and one Home/Far East commission (in the Far East January-December 1968) before she was paid off for disposal in August 1969.

DELIGHT's later career was brief. While in reserve she was towed from Devonport to Rosyth for an extensive refit. (September 1962-July 1964.) After recommissioning in July 1965 she spend two years with the 21st Escort Squadron, including a deployment to the Far East (January 1966-January 1967). She paid off for disposal in September 1967 after only 14 years, she was the first Daring to be scrapped. Her disarmed hulk arrived at Inverkeithing in December 1970.

HMS Diamond (May 1957)

Meanwhile DARING was out of service at Devonport for nearly seven years. At the end of 1966 she was recommissioned for one Far East deployment (July 1967-July 1968) and paid off at the end of 1968.

The AC group, originally to be the 7th DS, joined the Home Fleet between February 1952 and March 1954. Converting to General Service Commissions in 1954, the group completed two Home/Med. cycles by January 1959. They were overseas during the Suez crisis. Three served in the Med. while DIANA, which had been detached to the Far East in April 1956, operated in the Red Sea with the cruiser NEWFOUNDLAND. Further service in the Mediterranean followed, as the 5th Destroyer Squadron. They were on station September 1957-July 1958.

All four ships began a two year modernisation in January 1959. DECOY and DIANA at Devonport, DIAMOND at Chatham and DUCHESS at Portsmouth. During the course of this refit, both sets of torpedo tubes were removed, and facilities for the new "Seacat" missile incorporated. However, only DECOY was actually fitted with the missle. (From July 1960 until October 1962 she was based at Devonport as a trails ship for Seacat.) After a further refit, she joined the 21st Escort Squadron in April 1963. In the following two years she served with the Home Fleet and in the West Indies (April 1964-February 1965.) She was then refitted and placed in reserve at Portsmouth (March 1965-August 1967). A final two year commission saw DECOY in the Far East for the first time, (October 1968-September 1969.) She paid off in March 1970 — the last Daring in service — on her sale to Peru.

DUCHESS recommissioned in January 1961 as leader of the 5th Destroyer Squadron for service with the Home and Mediteranean Fleets. The squadron was in the Med. September 1961-May 1962. Her next commission was to be brief. Allocated to the new 24th Escort Squadron (formerly the 8th Destroyer Squadron) in the Far East in January 1963, after little more than a year on station she was transferred to Australia, replacing the lost VOYAGER. After eight years on loan to the Australian Navy she was purchased by them in 1972 (at scrap value) for conversion into a training ship in place of ANZAC.

In the 1960's DIANA was in commission longer than any other Daring — from January 1961 until her sale to Peru in October 1969. Apart from the first two years with the 5th Destroyer Squadron, she served, with few trips home, in the Far East from June 1963 until April 1969 in the 22nd and 24th Escort Squadrons and in the 1st and 2nd Destroyer Squadrons.

The first Daring completed was the last to remain in Royal Navy service. DIAMOND spent four years rotating between the Home and Med. Fleets, in the 5th DS and 23rd ES until January 1965. After more than two years in reserve at Chatham, she recommissioned for the last time in August 1967 and relieved DELIGHT in the Far East (July 1968-June 1969). When she paid off in December 1969 she was moored in Fareham Creek as Harbour Training ship for the COLLINGWOOD/SULTAN training establishments — in place of CROSSBOW. With the frigates BLACKWOOD (until 1974) and RUSSELL (since 1971) she performed a humble but useful role.

In 1981 she too headed for the scrapyard — the end of a class — and an era of World War 2 designed ships.

HMS Dainty (1968)

DARING CLASS

Displacement (tons) 2,800 **Length** 390 ft. **Beam** 43 ft. **Draught** 17 ft. (Max.) **Speed** 34¾ knots (as designed) **Armament** 6 x 4.5″ (in twin turrets, 2 forward, 1 aft); 6 x 40mm A.A. **Torpedo Tubes** 10 x 21″ (quintuple mountings). After bank of 5 was removed in 1958-59 and replaced by a deck-house. Forward mounting removed from "Dainty", "Daring", "Defender" and "Delight" in 1963-64. **A/S Weapons** squid mortar **Complement** 278-308

SHIP	BUILDERS	LAUNCH DATE
DECOY	Yarrow, Scotstoun	29-3-1949

Notes
Aug 1969 paid off at Portsmouth for disposal. 1969 sold to Peru renamed "Ferré" refitted by Cammell Laird, Birkenhead. 1971-73 another major refit. (Still in service 1980.)

SHIP	BUILDERS	LAUNCH DATE
DARING	Swan Hunter, Wallsend	10-8-1949

Notes
15 June 1971 arrived Blyth to be broken up.

SHIP	BUILDERS	LAUNCH DATE
DIAMOND	John Brown, Clydebank	14-6-1950

Notes
May 1963 suffered malicious damage at Chatham. 1970 replaced "Crossbow" as training ship for engine room personnel at Portsmouth. 1981 sold to be broken up on the Medway.

HMS Duchess (March 1956)

SHIP	BUILDERS	LAUNCH DATE
DEFENDER	Alex Stephen, Govan	27-7-1950

Notes
Sept 1969 paid off at Devonport for disposal. 1972 broken up at Inverkeithing.

SHIP	BUILDERS	LAUNCH DATE
DAINTY	J.S. White, Cowes	16-8-1950

Notes
31 July 1969 arrived Portsmouth to pay off for disposal. 1 Feb 1970 sold to be broken up at Cairnryan.

SHIP	BUILDERS	LAUNCH DATE
DELIGHT	Fairfield, Govan	21-12-1950

Notes
1971 broken up at Inverkeithing.

SHIP	BUILDERS	LAUNCH DATE
DUCHESS	J.I. Thornycroft Southampton	9-4-1951

Notes
1964 transferred to R.A.N. to replace HMAS Voyager lost a sea. 1972 purchased by R.A.N. 1977 de-commissioned — at Athol Bight — for disposal.

SHIP	BUILDERS	LAUNCH DATE
DIANA	Yarrow, Scotstoun	8.5.1952

Notes
1969 sold to Peru. Renamed "Palacios". Towed from Devonport to be refitted at Cammell Laird, Birkenhead. 1971-73 another major refit. (Still in service in 1980.)

HMS Diana

GUIDED MISSILE DESTROYERS
COUNTY CLASS

Displacement (tons) 5,200 **Length** 520 ft. 6 ins. **Beam** 54 ft. **Draught** 20 ft. (Max) **Speed** 32½ knots **Armament** 4 x 4.5" (two twin turrets forward) **Guided Missiles** 1 twin launcher "Seaslug" ship-to-air guided missiles on Quarterdeck. 2 quadruple launchers for "Seacat" close range ship-to-air missiles fitted abaft funnel. 3 Exocet in lieu of 2 x 4.5" guns in last 4 ships **Aircraft** 1 Westland Wessex Mk3 Helicopter carrying homing torpedoes. **Complement** 440.

SHIP	BUILDERS	LAUNCH DATE
DEVONSHIRE	Cammell Laird, Birkenhead	10-6-60

Notes
15 Nov 1962 First commissioned at the builder's yard. 1963 in Mediterranean. 1964 Far East. 28 July 1978 paid off at Portsmouth and placed on Disposal list. 1979 proposed sale to Egypt cancelled. 1982 laid up at Portsmouth awaiting disposal.

SHIP	BUILDERS	LAUNCH DATE
HAMPSHIRE	John Brown, Clydebank	16-3-1961

Notes
15 March 1963 First commissioned at the builder's yard. March-Dec 1964 Far East. April 1976 Paid off. 25 April 1979 towed from Chatham to Briton Ferry to be broken up.

SHIP	BUILDERS	LAUNCH DATE
KENT	Harland & Wolff, Belfast	27-9-1961

Notes
15 Aug 1963 First commissioned at Belfast. 1964-65 Far East. 29 Nov 1976 damaged by fire whilst refitting at Portsmouth. Oct 1978 arrived Wallsend-on-Tyne for refit. July 1980 relieved "FIFE" as Harbour Training Ship at Portsmouth.

Two of a kind at Malta

HMS London (1970)

HMS Glamorgan (April 1977)

SHIP	BUILDERS	LAUNCH DATE
LONDON	Swan Hunter, Wallsend	7-12-61

Notes
14 Nov 1963 first commissioned at builder's yard. 1965 Far East. Dec 1981 fired last broadside in R.N. on passage to Portsmouth to pay off for disposal. Jan 1982 sold to Pakistan.

SHIP	BUILDERS	LAUNCH DATE
FIFE	Fairfield, Govan	9-7-1964

Notes
21 June 1966 First commissioned. Nov 1979 After major rescue operation in Dominica after a hurricane, she became Harbour Training Ship at Portsmouth until commencement of refit in July 1980.

SHIP	BUILDERS	LAUNCH DATE
GLAMORGAN	Vickers, Tyne	9-7-1964

Notes
14 Oct 1966 first commissioned at builder's yard. April 1968 left Portsmouth for Far East Commission.

SHIP	BUILDERS	LAUNCH DATE
ANTRIM	Fairfield, Govan	19-10-1967

Notes
23 Nov 1970 handed over to R.N. at Portsmouth.

SHIP	BUILDERS	LAUNCH DATE
NORFOLK	Swan Hunter, Wallsend	16-11-1967

Notes
7 March 1970 — First commissioned. 17 Feb 1982 sailed for Chile with UK/Chilean crew having been sold as a defence economy. Renamed "Prat".

HMS Antrim (Apr 1975)

TYPE 82

Displacement (tons) 6,100 **Length** 507 ft. **Beam** 55 ft. **Draught** 16 ft. 8 ins. **Speed** 29 knots **Aircraft** launching platform only for one helicopter **Missiles** Sea Dart (twin launchers) **A/S Weapons** Ikara single launcher forward **Guns** 1 x 4.5″; 2 x 20mm **Complement** 407

SHIP	BUILDERS	LAUNCH DATE
BRISTOL	Swan Hunter, Wallsend	30-6-1969

Notes
31 March 1973 commissioned at Avonmouth. 1 Nov 1974 damaged by fire in steam turbine and boiler compartments at Milford Haven. 1976-77 refit and repairs.

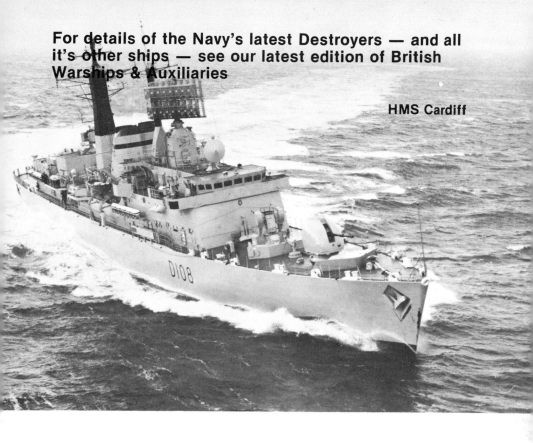

For details of the Navy's latest Destroyers — and all it's other ships — see our latest edition of British Warships & Auxiliaries

HMS Cardiff

ALPHABETICAL LIST OF SHIPBUILDERS

Wm. BEARDMORE & Co., Dalmuir.
John BROWN & Co. Ltd., Clydebank, Glasgow.
Cammell LAIRD & Co. Ltd., Birkenhead and Tranmere.
Wm. DENNY & Bros. Ltd., Dumbarton.
Wm. DOXFORD & Sons, Sunderland.
FAIRFIELD Shipbuilding & Engineering Co. Ltd., Govan, Glasgow.
HARLAND & Wolff Ltd., Belfast.
R. & W. HAWTHORN Leslie & Co. Ltd., Hebburn-on-Tyne.
PALMERS Shipbuilding & Iron Co., Hebburn-on-Tyne.
SCOTTS Shipbuilding & Engineering Co. Ltd., Greenock.
ALEX STEPHEN & Sons Ltd., Linthouse, Govan, Glasgow.
SWAN HUNTER & Wigham Richardson Ltd., Wallsend-on-Tyne.
John I. THORNYCROFT & Co. Ltd., Woolston, Southampton.
(later VOSPER Thornycroft (UK) Ltd.)
VICKERS Armstrong, Barrow-in-Furness.
VICKERS Armstrong, Newcastle-on-Tyne.
J. Samuel WHITE & Co. Ltd., Cowes, I.O.W.
YARROW & Co. Ltd., Scotstoun, Glasgow.

PHOTOGRAPHS

I am most grateful for the help received from Mr Sid Goodman of Plymouth for his help researching many of these photographs.

Photographs of ships taken pre-1945 are deliberately included to show how ships looked "when new"—and to show how they were rebuilt after the war—often completely changing their outline.

The photographs on Pages 7, 8, 9, 11, 12, 46, 49, 61, 62, 63, 71, 82, 88, 90, 95, (bottom), 97, 99, 100 (top), 101, 102, 106, 109 (top), 111 (bottom), 114 (top), 117, 119 (top), 120, 121, 123, 139, 141, 142, 143 are Offical Royal Navy pictures.

Those on Pages 1, 21, 25, 33, 72, 78, 79, 84, 87, 89, 100 (bottom), 103, 109 (bottom), 111 (top), 116, 125 (bottom), 137 are reproduced by permission of the Imperial War Museum.

My thanks to Mr Laurence Phillips for permission to use his photograph on Page 86 and Mr P.A. Vicary on Page 47.

The remaining photos are from the Wright & Logan collection from whom copies are available (20, Queen Street, Portsmouth).

INDEX